The Dysfunctional Organization:
Why we will never be competitive in America again

Ron Emery

ACKNOWLEDGMENTS

Thanks to all who have believed in me over the years, through life's ups and downs: my wife and kids, who through their thoughtful ribbing, have gotten me to think and see opportunities where others did not.?
Thanks to my mentors, who have made a big difference in how I see the world today. Thanks to Doug, who helped with some of the research and ideas, and to Steve, who have helped with pieces of the book I could not have completed by myself.

TABLE OF CONTENTS

ACKNOWLEDGMENTS   **III**

TABLE OF CONTENTS   **5**

INTRODUCTION   **7**

CHAPTER 1:   **16**

HOW AMERICA'S MONETARY POLICIES HAVE HURT US OVER THE LAST 50 YEARS

CHAPTER 2:   **35**

AMERICA'S CONVOLUTED TRADE POLICIES AND HOW THEY HAVE HURT THE ECONOMY

3 THE WALMARTING OF AMERICA   **52**

4 THE LABOR MISPERCEPTION   **68**

5 THE LOSS OF INDIVIDUALISM AND THE AGE OF GENERIC MANAGEMENT   **85**

6 WHERE HAVE ALL THE LEADERS GONE?   **99**

7 "I CALLED TO TELL YOU YOU'RE FIRED"   **115**

8 WHY OUR MBAS FAIL   **134**

CONCLUSION: WHAT DO WE DO NOW?
     152

REFERENCES   **1657**

INTRODUCTION:
HOW DID WE GET HERE?

The Dysfunctional Organization

Introduction

I did not start writing this book to create one of the world's greatest pieces of literature, and by the way, I am positive it won't be received that way. I am not that naive. I am, however writing because I think it is important. Everyone should consider it important as well. You may not like what I say but I have put thirty years of business resolve out there to review.

I am concerned, however, about our communities, our state, our country, and our world. I am concerned about your grandchildren and my potential grandchildren. I am concerned about our leadership position in the world and its dwindling significance. I am concerned about fairness and giving everyone the opportunity to live the American dream. I am concerned about the growing hopeless underclass that we have created by our lack of concern for their welfare, as well as our inability to produce jobs to give them the opportunities they deserve. I am very concerned about how the economic engine is driven to provide jobs and produce goods and services that are of tremendous value to a thriving and growing economy, and how our children can survive in such a world. In other words, I would like to leave this earth in better shape than it was when I arrived, just like you all would.

This is not a traditional organizational development book. Neither is it a traditional business strategy book. Rather, it is a compilation of what I have seen over thirty years of being an executive in an organization, getting fed up with the status quo, and becoming amazed at the traditional organization's inability to get out of its own way. I can't necessarily say these are bad organizations, but they are run in such an incestuous manner that they can't help themselves.

Why are they so dysfunctional, you might ask? There are a number of reasons...

Organizations pride themselves on promoting from within. They take the most senior welder and make him the foreman. They say, "This guy doesn't have the skills to lead a team, but we will make him the foreman, and he'll accomplish the job. Let's take a senior engineer, who is a great engineer, and let's make him the president of our North American business." This engineer is a survivor. Yes, he has made it through the last thirty years of consolidation, but only because business was so lousy that the best people left. Now we are left with a good engineer who is way over his head and shouldn't be leading the organization, but we trust him. So again we settle for mediocrity. Let's take our brightest accountant and make him the supervisor of other accountants but they really haven't been trained as leaders or managers. We haven't given him or her the tools to do the best job possible

Why do we continue to take the safe path rather than find the right individual who can lead us to the next level? We are dysfunctional. This is dysfunctional management, or to broaden it, a dysfunctional organization.

We continue to lobby the government for protectionism rather than lean out and automate our organizations. Now, I will not argue that sometimes we are at an unfair disadvantage and the government should rescue us, but I will argue that most times this disadvantage is because we refuse to see our own inadequacies and change. Most of you would agree that our elected officials and the folks within our governments are not the most flexible, accommodating, and willing to change. Just spend a Saturday morning at your local DMV and see if it doesn't raise your blood pressure just a bit. Why go ask them for help when they caused most of our problems by not understanding trade policies, or in fact, any policy they actually installed?

I make my living by fixing broken businesses. I have been successful at it, and I love doing it. My friends joke that I will never run out of work because there is "no shortage of broken businesses." I have spent the last thirty years working on businesses that just did not work quite right. Maybe they did not make enough money to invest back into the business to make it successful; maybe they were run by generational owners who lost the entrepreneurial touch that their grandpas had when they started the venture. Maybe they just didn't work from an organizational standpoint. Maybe the leaders of those businesses had such large egos they stymied every positive attribute of their companies. There are many reasons for failure.

But to me, failure is never an option. I have done a lot of work for a large multinational that everyone would recognize. It is a very successful organization in some respects, but even there they can't see the forest for the trees. It is not that they are inept or lack vision, but when you can only look at a problem with the set of eyes that got you into the fix to begin with, you can't see exactly how to extricate yourself from it.

So back to the question of how we got here. The answer is not easy; in fact, it is rather complex, and many people share the blame. I will try to address some of these issues in this essay: Our government and our lack of ability to understand simple economic and trade terms is one of them. Our failing schools is another. Our world being built on labor in the past, and us not valuing it anymore, is a third.

When I was younger, which must seem like centuries ago to my children, we had shop classes. They taught us mechanical drawing and how to work with electrical equipment, wood, and metal. Now, I must agree that I wasn't very good in any of those. That is why I chose college, since I could only make a living with my head, not my hands. I admire those who have skills with their hands, however, and maybe it is because I lack those skills. They can do a lot that I cannot do. We need tool makers, we need electricians, we need carpenters and laborers as well. A solid education in the trades is very valuable today, and we lack those skills. A strong manufacturing society needs those skills, so how do we get them back?

The simple answer is, we do it through trade schools and through our high schools teaching our youths good, skilled jobs that pay a livable wage as well. Our universities have failed us by focusing on research rather than giving our young a toolset that they can use the rest of their lives. Our business schools, in particular have failed us. They seem to insist that practical experience and hands on learning have no purpose today. That is precisely why they have failed. Most people learn by doing. The structure of our businesses, and how we reward conformity rather than creativity, has failed us. We have really failed this generation because of our lack of vision and preparedness. We have made it tougher for our kids to compete in this world, and we have made it especially tough for our grandchildren.

I could write a separate book on the bosses I have had, and how they felt the need to protect their turf, and how they used lying and deceit to gain an advantage over others. Management traditionally hasn't been in it for the success of all. Management is the problem. Labor, typically is not the problem. Management is being taught in the business schools, and greed and excess are rampant. There is no possible reason a CEO today should be compensated at $50 million, but it happens. The educator of today in our business schools must be a doer (practitioner) and not a researcher. Practitioners should be the ones teaching our MBAs.

There is an evolving value system in America today. We expect to pay less for everything when we go to Walmart, and Walmart complies, but we also expect our wages to continue to rise. That is not logical to me. If I expect to pay less, I have to expect my wages to go down, not up. Why do we not value individuals anymore? When have we become so collective? You will see what I mean when you read the chapters in front of you.

So the fact of the matter is, we are here. Now, where do we go from here?

CHAPTER 1:
HOW AMERICA'S MONETARY
POLICIES HAVE HURT US OVER THE
LAST 50 YEARS

The Dysfunctional Organization

The Dysfunctional Organization

<u>Chapter 1</u>

Just three hours before midnight, on December 31st of 2012, congress came to an agreement on amendments to the Budget Control Act of 2011 that was to go into effect at the beginning of 2013. The act was slated to place restrictions on government spending as well as increases on taxation that, while decreasing the national deficit by $560 billion, would most certainly send the U.S. economy into a recession. In the final hours of 2012, congress initiated some changes that would most likely prevent recession, but would do little in the way of decreasing the deficit. (Trotman, 2013) As of the beginning of 2013, the U.S. federal budget deficit was about a trillion dollars, with the national debt being about 16 trillion dollars. (*National Debt Awareness Center*, 2013)

The United States is in severe debt—two to three times higher than any other country—and it seems that the only way to get out of it is through recession or possibly even depression. In the meantime, the U.S. dollar is diminishing in its share of the global economy, and emerging markets such as China and India are rising in the global financial markets. As financial crises, such as the fiscal cliff of 2013, continue to occur, the U.S. dollar is losing relative trust in the eyes of these emerging markets as well as elsewhere.

The phrase we see on our money, "Backed by the full faith and credit of the U.S. government" doesn't hold quite as much weight as it used to, and it may hold even less going into the future. The U.S. dollar is backed by nothing but a promise. When that promise ceases to be believed, its value ceases to exist.

This tremendously affects the way organizations today operate. Every business runs on cash, and the most important financial term today is "cash flow." Needless to say, the most important people in our businesses today are not the CEOs but the CFOs (Chief Financial Officers). William Fuessler, (2010) in an article for Forbes, says that,

> "The global economic downturn has put a bright spotlight on chief financial officers and the finance organizations they preside over. Amid all the world's volatility and uncertainty, they have been drawn ever more often into the boardroom discussions, where decisions are made. Their bosses, chief executive officers, no longer want mere number crunchers; they want them to provide forecasts, manage risks, and provide insight

into issues ranging from pricing to production. As a result, CFOs are emerging with far greater clout and responsibilities than before."

IBM's new 2010 Global CFO Study, based on input from more than 1,900 CFOs and senior finance leaders worldwide, attests to this shift. Although the importance of core finance tasks hasn't diminished in any way, CFOs have had to sharply increase their focus on company-wide concerns. The IBM study indicates that they are seriously struggling to come to terms with the dramatically altered economic landscape, and only half of those surveyed said they feel they're effective in giving their CEOs adequate business insight. An overwhelming majority are planning big changes."

This changes CFOs' role in their organizations substantially. They are now involved as risk assessors and risk managers, more than ever before, to control the financial health of the organization. What does this mean to the organization, you might ask? It means, a significant sense of control goes to the financial folks in all planning aspects of the business.

Fuessler goes on to call the CFO's role evolving into that of a "value integrator".

"Value integrators also have far greater analytical capabilities, enabling them to generate business insights that can help them spot market opportunities, react faster, and ultimately predict changes in the business environment. They've even figured out how to drive sustained business outcomes in times of market instability.

That's the kind of commitment and vision it takes to become a value integrator. How can a CFO get started on the journey? There's no one-size-fits-all method; it varies from organization to organization. But you can start by asking these few key questions:

• –Do I have all the information I need from all parts of the enterprise at all times?

• –Is the company focused on the right business metrics, the ones that truly drive business performance?

• –How accurate are our crucial forecasts, such as the ones for customer demand and unit costs?

• –Does the organization have sufficient

analytical skills?

The answers to these questions will start to point a CFO to gaps in his or her finance organization, and awareness of those gaps will guide the creation of an action plan—an absolutely crucial activity that must be undertaken with great care, as the decisions made for it will have great ramifications down the road."

These are great skills to have in an organization, but they do take away from its entrepreneurial spirit. Under this philosophy, the organization becomes a gigantic financial machine, focused simply on shareholder value retention, and not willing to take nearly as many risks as they did previously. So currency is becoming devalued and the organization is focusing on shareholder value, which means there is a tremendous push to drive labor costs and fixed costs lower.

Where do they turn to do this? They say, "Let's drive labor costs and all of the associated costs downward by shifting production offshore." This is an organizational fallacy. Labor, typically is not a large percentage of their costs, but it might be the easiest resource to outsource, so they move ahead, pushing labor dollars at first to the Southern US, South America, and the Caribbean, and then on to Japan, Taiwan, China, India, and finally to Viet Nam. Where will they go next? When will we run out of countries willing to drive labor costs to a minimum? We will discuss this more in the labor misperception chapter.

For thousands of years, various commodities have been widely accepted as currencies among various groups. As a more efficient system to bartering, coinage backed by commodities such as silver and gold has arisen throughout human history as forms of economic exchange. According to the United States Mint, in 1792 the United States issued the Mint and Coinage Act, setting up the silver dollar as the principal mode of U.S. currency, establishing the decimal system of denominations, and creating a fixed-ratio of gold to the U.S. dollar. In subsequent decades, the gold standard went through various iterations in the U.S. until 1968, when the dollar ceased to be backed by any commodity and became, like much of the world's currency, fiat money.

Fiat Money is defined by economist Greg Mankiw (2011) in this way: "Fiat money, such as paper dollars, is money without intrinsic value: It would be worthless if it were not used as money." All major currencies in the world today consist of fiat money—money backed by governments but holding no value apart from the value attributed to it by governments. The U.S. dollar bill only has value because of the phrase printed on it: "This note is legal tender for all debts, public and private." Commodities such as silver and gold are not fiat money and need no such validation; they have globally-recognized intrinsic value.

The primary reason for deviation from the gold standard is said to be its inflexibility and lack of liquidity. Gold is not as easily converted to cash as is fiat currency. Moreover, there is a fixed amount of gold in the world, so it has been suggested that a gold standard could inhibit global economic growth. Using the gold standard prevents governments from using inflationary monetary policy to stimulate growth and increase the wealth of its citizens.

In his extensive history of the gold standard, *Gold: The Once and Future Money*, Nathan Lewis (2007) suggests that for much of history, a single, global monetary system was not so unusual. "A gold standard among multiple countries is, in essence, a world currency," he says. "It needs no central governing bodies; it is not dependent on any sort of fiscal rules and restrictions; and any country that chooses to participate may do so unilaterally. It is the citizen's world currency."

Lewis continues, "There are those today who argue for a world currency, as if this were some sort of far-off Utopian ideal like a unified world government. In fact, the world had a common currency for centuries and discarded it only three decades ago." Finally he adds, "Under the gold standard, the gold market is an open market free of government manipulation."

In recent years, there has been a revival of interest in the gold standard. Many, specifically those aligned with Austrian economics and libertarianism, have proposed a renewed gold standard. Fiat money has given government leaders the power to exercise control over their citizens through spending power created through monetary policy. While many economists are wary of the inflexibility of the gold standard and the limitations in places on economic growth, the risk of giving a central bank too much power may be even greater.

If a gold standard were to be reinstated, how would it affect how we spend money in the U.S.? According to Lewis Lehrman (2011), author of *The New Gold Standard*, nothing will change about the way we interact with the marketplace, except our confidence in the interactions. The gold standard,

Lehrman explains, "means that the American government defines its currency as a fixed amount of gold of a certain weight and purity. Under a gold standard you could go into the bank and bring in a tenth of an ounce value of gold—say $100 under a gold standard—and receive a $100 gold coin.

Alternatively, you could bring in that gold coin and either deposit it in your bank or checking account receiving a deposit credit for $100 convertible to an ounce of gold on demand or get $100 in gold certificates (paper money)." Acceptance of the gold standard would not mean that we actually use gold, but only that we are aware of the fact that we can redeem our currency for gold should we choose to do so.

Lehrman goes on to argue why we need to revert to the gold standard in America:

> The gold standard is real money, acceptable from time immemorial, ruling out substantial and sustained deflation and inflation. The gold standard leads at home to peaceful cooperation and trade among diverse citizens. The international gold standard is the optimum non-national world currency, which leads to cooperation among different

sovereign countries and distinct cultures. Convertible currencies are the least imperfect vehicles inducing cooperation of competing interests, because, despite all national differences, each sovereign national currency is convertible to a neutral, common world currency – a specified weight unit of gold. Thus all currencies convertible to gold are mutually convertible to each other. Such an international monetary standard is beyond the control of any one country. *The Lehrman Institute*, 2013)

Adopting the gold standard would simplify exchange rates and base the world economy on something fixed and less dependent on the whims of government bureaucrats.

Not only would a return to the gold standard renew faith in U.S. currency and make it more competitive in the global economy, but it would also alleviate much of the obscurity in the monetary system. Citizens would be more confident in their currency and would be more willing to work harder to generate more wealth. Innovation is stifled by lack of faith in the rewards for one's efforts. Faith in the U.S. dollar is not only declining globally; it is also declining domestically: Americans fear what their money will be worth in the future.

So, what does all this mean for business? In short, it means increased risk. The more volatility there is in the stability of currency, the riskier it is to start business ventures, launch new products, hire employees, and purchase capital. In a speech given on September 17, 2011 in Zurich, Switzerland, economist Hans Hermann Hoppes (2011) made the following statement: "The existence of a state, then, heightens the uncertainty facing the businessman. It makes the future less certain than would be the case otherwise. Realizing this, many people who might otherwise become businessmen will not become businessmen at all. And many businessmen will see their business plans spoiled. Not because they did not correctly anticipate future consumer demand, but because the physical basis, on which their plan was based, was altered by some unexpected and unanticipated change in state laws and regulations." In other words, when the value of money is arbitrarily controlled by government officials, the business person has less of an incentive to engage in behaviors that involve high financial risk.

When entrepreneurs and those with entrepreneurial mindsets lose the incentive to take risks, our economy goes right to the brink of failure. It is difficult enough for those in business to predict consumer demand of products and services, let alone whether or not the value of their money is going to be the same.

The U.S. government will probably never return to a gold standard, despite the underground movement to reinstate it. The financial system in the U.S. has become far too elaborate to unravel. My intention is to warn you, as you probably are already aware, of the increased challenges you face in the fiat money system. As the national debt continues to grow and the hopes of decreasing the deficit diminish, the situation is likely to only get worse. But there is one country who got it right—Germany.

Stephen Rattner (2011)describes Germany's renaissance in an article for *Foreign Affairs Magazine*. He says:

> When it comes to boosting exports, of course, the need to maintain or even increase the size of the manufacturing sector, in particular, has been an article of faith in major developed countries for decades. Politicians and voters alike believe that having companies that "make something" is a key element of

economic success, in part because manufacturing jobs have historically paid above-average wages. For its part, Germany embraced manufacturing, and much of its economic success is thanks to that decision.

THE MITTELSTAND MIRACLE

Germans credit both their public and their private sectors for their country's success. Germany's government, particularly under Gerhard Schröder, who was chancellor from 1998 to 2005, played an important role in the country's economic growth. In early 2005, Schröder pushed through parliament a massive reform program called Agenda 2010. Doing so was politically costly for the chancellor. His party suffered a major loss in that spring's regional election, and when Schröder called for an early general election in the fall that year, he was defeated. But Agenda 2010 survived and successfully rolled back the German welfare state by, among other things, paring unemployment benefits to encourage work, relaxing stultifying regulatory practices, and forging a grand bargain with labor unions whereby the unions agreed to hold down wages and the government assured job security for workers.

This greater job security was afforded in large measure through a "short work" scheme: workers' total number of hours were reduced to avoid layoffs, and the government covered part of their lost salaries. Approximately 1.5 million Germans were enrolled in the program at its peak, in May 2009, at a cost to the government of 4.6 billion euros that year alone. According to a 2009 report by the Organization for Economic Cooperation and Development, the program saved approximately 500,000 jobs during the recent economic recession.

Of at least equal importance was the role of the private sector, especially the innumerable small and medium-sized manufacturing firms known as the *Mittelstand*. These companies combine the advantages of stable family ownership with a focus on producing sophisticated goods that emerging markets cannot easily replicate. As Germans like to say, "We make the thing that goes inside the thing that goes inside the thing." Although family-owned businesses can be a mixed blessing, of course—they are subject to familial strife and succession problems—the overall success of these companies is widely acknowledged. The *Mittelstand* now employ millions of people and seem to put a higher priority on employing Germans than do publicly traded multinational giants. Many Germans believe that since the *Mittelstand* are privately owned, they focus more on long-term growth than short-term profits.

A significant portion of Germany's industrial success can be traced to two manufacturing sectors. The first, heavily dominated by the *Mittelstand*, includes companies that build the sophisticated machine tools that emerging markets need as they develop their own manufacturing capabilities. This might sound like selling arms to one's adversary, but it has worked well for Germany. The second sector includes Germany's marquee auto brands -- BMW, Daimler, Porsche, Audi, and the like. Automakers are, of course, central to the German economy, composing about 20 percent of GDP. In particular, high-end cars have become hot commodities for affluent consumers in booming new markets, such as China, which alone accounts for 25 percent of BMW's global profits."

Some have warned that Germany's economy is overly export-dependent and vulnerable to the vicissitudes of the global economy, but the country's success as an global power is unparalleled from an economic perspective. There are some lessons that we—individual Americans as well as our organizations— can learn from the *Mittelstand* Miracle.

Now put all of these facts together:

1. We left the gold standard and are not likely to return. As the global economies grow and we source more from third world countries, our standard of living drops because our currency becomes less valuable.

2. Our organizations' focus on risk mitigation through the financial office and devaluation of currency is certainly a risk. Our organizations today are acting less entrepreneurial and more like conservative risk managers, so they take less chances and are focused on keeping shareholder value intact.

3. The Federal Reserve Bank lives in this cloaked identity, not controlled by any branch of government,

making monetary policies and printing money so that our dollar is devalued continuously. In order to drive our economy forward we have manipulated borrowing rates, in a true test of "voodoo economics," which cannot last forever. This forces our organizations to be risk mitigators rather than creative spirits making our lives easier and more fulfilled.

This is one reason our organizations are dysfunctional.

CHAPTER 2:
AMERICA'S CONVOLUTED TRADE POLICIES AND HOW THEY HAVE HURT THE ECONOMY

The Dysfunctional Organization

Chapter 2

In his classic work, *Principles of Political Economy and Taxation*, originally published in 1817, economist David Ricardo famously makes the case for free trade:

> Under a system of perfectly free commerce, each country naturally devotes its capital and labour to such employments as are most beneficial to each. This pursuit of individual advantage is admirably connected with the universal good of the whole. By stimulating industry, by regarding ingenuity, and by using most efficaciously the peculiar powers bestowed by nature, it distributes labour most effectively and most economically.

There is an idea floating around in the mainstream media that needs to be cleared up. "Free trade" isn't the problem. "Free trade" isn't why we're losing jobs to China and why entire industries are collapsing in the U.S. In fact, although the United States may be the freest-trading country in the world, it is precisely because it isn't free enough that we are having many of the problems we are having. One of the problems with free trade is the fact it is not evenly applied around the globe. It isn't evenly applied in the US. It is policy written into trade laws that keeps American companies from employing Americans.

There are many books written on the pros and cons of free trade and, although I am an advocate of free trade, it is not my intention to make this book an argument for freer trade. Rather than calling attention to the benefits of free trade, I would rather focus on the realities of free trade. In his contemporary classic, *The World is Flat*, New York Times journalist Thomas Friedman (2005) explains 10 world-flatteners that have led to the globalized world in which we are now living:

1. The fall of the Berlin Wall, and the subsequent victory of Capitalism over Communism.
2. The Initial Public Offering of web browser Netscape and the ensuing global connectivity.
3. The introduction of workflow software and its impact on fluid activity within organizations.
4. The introduction of the open source movement of global collaboration with blogs and wikis.
5. The trend for organizations to begin

outsourcing jobs to other companies.

6. The trend for organizations to begin offshoring jobs to other countries.

7. The revolution in supply chain management with growing technology that enabled seamless collaboration throughout the value chain.

8. The technological growth that empowered the individual and the small business to compete globally.

9. The superfluity of information available from the web and the ease of access via search engines and news sites.

10. The exponential leap in processing power of information technology, enabling the emergence of technologies such as VoIP, video conferencing, and mobile computing.

There are industries, once thriving, that don't even exist today in America. The clothing industry, as late as the 1950's, was thriving in America. Little by little, in the search for the lower almighty labor dollar the production of clothing shifted to the southern states and eventually offshore. Remember that this kind of manufacturing was an economic staple of small New England towns that brought us all the famous names we wore as kids or young adults. The same thing happened in the watch industry, textile industry, the bicycle manufacturing industry and the shoe industry and many other industries following them. Why was it cheaper to make things offshore than to make them in America? The answer is simple, our trade laws were never written to protect us as much as they were written to exploit us.

You see, back when America was the king of manufacturing, we had technology and infrastructure that no other nation in the world had. And our economy was a growing engine we had to feed. Two world wars that were not on our continent helped us immensely keeping people busy and providing for opportunities for all. The shift happened slowly after World War Two, as Germany and Japan were rebuilt. Liberal trade policies with both facilitated new markets in America for their goods. Cheap toys flooded the markets from Japan and automobiles from Germany. Their internal markets grew, which allowed them to invest. The Japanese understood that quality was key to their growth and developed some pretty remarkable vehicles, just as America was getting tired and complacent.

Textiles, shoes, watches, and clothing all moved offshore and still the American economic machine roared. America gradually shifted its focus from an economy focused on manufactured goods and moved toward a service economy model. Everywhere on the landscape *Holiday Inns* popped up. The hospitality (service) industry was born, Americans with more discretionary income invested in the stock market (again a move toward the service economy), and insurance to protect what they owned, as well as the banking industry, began to boom.

The food industry boomed as well; America's farms were the breadbasket of the world, as we grew much more food than we consumed, so these markets became ready trading partners for our farmers and the food processing industry. The restaurant industry grew at an exponential pace as a result—especially fast food restaurants. We forgot about our manufacturing edge. See, it would have been difficult to put tariffs on imported steel because we wouldn't have been allowed to put the McDonalds or Burger King in Japan or China. The service industry grew at a rapid rate even as manufacturing fell behind.

But steel production didn't fall behind in Europe or Brazil; they were investing in the latest technological upgrades and producing good quality steel at a low price. We did not invest here in the Americas, and as a result, in the late seventies, there was a huge collapse. I remember it well. I had just graduated from high school and remember "Black Monday" in Youngstown, Ohio.

Jamison Cocklin, of *The Vindicator* (2013) (Youngstown's newspaper) talks about it decades later in an article:

> There are no easy words to describe what happened 35 years ago, when thousands of employees learned their livelihoods would disappear. A sense of devastation is how those who lived through the ordeal recall it. On Sept. 19, 1977, Jennings R. Lambeth, president of Youngstown Sheet & Tube Co., made a shocking announcement that the company would shutter its Campbell Works in Campbell and Struthers. Between the two locations, 4,100 workers made a living and provided for themselves and their families. For many, the industry was all they knew. That day, known in the Mahoning Valley as Black Monday, eventually cost 5,000 workers their jobs, and marked the official beginning of a death-spiral for the Valley's steel mills. All told, more than 40,000 would lose their jobs in the coming decade.

This was devastating news for this mid-sized town in northeastern Ohio, but this isn't just one isolated story. There are many Youngstowns being repeated all over the eastern United States. How did it happen? I suppose, with the shift to the global economy it was bound to.

In an age of increasing globalization, with cultural values intersecting more and more as the years go by, it is rather silly to hold to protectionist ideas. Protectionism, is by all accounts a means of protecting ones interest without the concern of one's neighbor. Free trade is inevitable and it is only going to get freer; the question should be about what kind of policy we create within the context of free trade. The debate seems to be constantly centered around free trade versus protectionism. Should we allow domestic companies to purchase capital and labor from overseas, or should we enforce domestic purchasing alone? Some would point out the increased outsourcing of labor to countries such as China and India and find a correlation with the downfall of manufacturing in the U.S. While it is clear that outsourcing jobs to other countries has played a role in the decline of American industries, I would argue that it is the specific policy involved in outsourcing that is really to blame.

Tariffs, or taxes on imports, are going to exist just as sure as free trade will. Politicians have an incentive to at least appear as if they are protecting the interests of their citizens. So, politicians in the U.S. enact tariffs on goods purchased from outside of the U.S. under the guise of protecting the U.S. economy by favoring businesses within the United States. But the particular products on which tariffs are placed can make a huge difference between a trade policy that facilitates economic growth and a trade policy that destroys it. Most of the world seems to use the tariff idea to their advantage. We here in America do not do it so much for manufacturing.

Richard McCormack, in an article entitled, "The Plight of American Manufacturing," published in *The American Prospect*, (2009) tells us:

>"Long before the banking collapse of 2008, such important U.S. industries as machine tools, consumer electronics, auto parts, appliances, furniture, telecommunications equipment, and many others that had once dominated the global marketplace suffered their own economic collapse. Manufacturing employment dropped to 11.7 million in October 2009, a loss of 5.5 million or 32

percent of all manufacturing jobs since October 2000. The last time fewer than 12 million people worked in the manufacturing sector was in 1941. In October 2009, more people were officially unemployed (15.7 million) than were working in manufacturing.

When a factory closes, it creates a vortex that has far-reaching consequences. The Milken Institute estimates that every computer-manufacturing job in California creates 15 jobs outside the factory. Close a manufacturing plant, and a supply chain of producers disappears with it. Dozens of companies get hurt: those supplying computer-aided design and business software; automation and robotics equipment, packaging, office equipment and supplies; telecommunications services; energy and water utilities; research and development, marketing and sales support; and building and equipment maintenance and janitorial services. The burden spreads to local restaurants, cultural establishments, shopping outlets, and then to the tax base that supports police, firemen, schoolteachers, and libraries.

Has U.S. manufacturing declined because its

companies are not competitive? Hardly. American companies are among the most efficient in the world. The nation's steel industry, for instance, produces 1 ton of steel using two man-hours. A comparable ton of steel in China is produced with 12 man-hours, and Chinese companies produce three times the amount of carbon emissions per ton of steel. The same kinds of comparisons are true for other industries.

But American companies have difficulty competing against foreign countries that undervalue their currencies, pay health care for their workers; provide subsidies for energy, land, buildings, and equipment; grant tax holidays and rebates and provide zero-interest financing; pay their workers poverty wages that would be illegal in the United States, and don't enforce safety or environmental regulations.

Proponents of free trade and outsourcing argue that the United States remains the largest manufacturing economy in the world. Yet, total manufacturing—gross domestic product—in 2008 (at $1.64 trillion) represented 11.5 percent of U.S. economic output, down from 17 percent in 1999, and 28 percent in 1959. As for our balance of trade, U.S. imports of goods totaled $2.52 trillion in 2008, while exports came to $1.29 trillion -- creating a goods deficit of $821 billion. Those imported goods represented 17.6 percent of U.S. GDP. The U.S. trade deficit in goods and services in 2008 stood at $700 billion -- or more than $2,000 for every American.

That is pretty scary stuff, especially when you look at the free use of global tariffs to protect every other industry.

The United States uses a system of placing taxes on imports called The Harmonized Tariff Schedule (International Trade Commission, 2013). Within this document, the U.S. policy makers iron out exactly what materials and products taxes are placed on during import. The guiding principle is that taxes are placed on all products except those intended for final sale in the U.S. That is, taxes are placed on imports of components for products that will be manufactured in the U.S. or modified in some way before entering the marketplace.

Let's look at one example. Hewlett-Packard outsources the assembly of the majority of its computers and other products to China. But why does it do this? Is it because American labor is too expensive? Is it because Chinese labor is such a bargain? Not exactly. HP could assemble the products in America if it weren't for trade policies preventing them from doing so. In order to assemble the products in the U.S., HP would have to pay trade duties on each of the components when importing them into the country. However, if the company has the products assembled in China, where the components are purchased, HP doesn't have to pay duties on the finished product. As we can see, arbitrary trade policies in the U.S. are directly incentivizing U.S. manufacturing companies to use foreign labor to build their products.

Let's look at a country that does not have such a policy. Germany does the opposite of U.S. by imposing trade duties on the final products rather than on the components. As a result, German companies are incentivized to buy materials outside of Germany but employ workers inside of Germany to assemble them. If we look at the data, we'll find that Germany was the largest net exporter in 2011. Doesn't it make more sense to impose duties on finished products rather than on components? That's how we can keep Americans employed within in the

context of free trade—crafting policies that
incentivize companies to give jobs to Americans.

So, that is the climate in which you are operating
while doing business in America. You are penalized
for hiring domestic workers to manufacture products
with materials purchased from international sources.
The problem is that average citizens, policy-makers,
and even business leaders seem to be oblivious to this
obvious flaw in the trade policy. In 2011, General
Electric CEO Jeffrey Immelt proposed that American
manufacturing companies hire more engineers in the
U.S. Immelt argued that, "when taking into account
the costs of shipping products made overseas back
into the US, the profit margins associated with
outsourcing are no longer large enough to justify
depriving middle class Americans these jobs.
Corporations need to take into account where they
create jobs and how this affects consumer markets,
considering outsourcing is taking income away from
the same people that are the consumers for most of
these company's products." (Broyles, 2012) There
may be some truth to this claim, but it completely
ignores the fact that American manufacturing
executives are inhibited by the arbitrary trade policies.

Indeed, in his recent book *The Great Rebalancing*,
financial economist Michael Pettis (2013) argues that

the recent financial crisis was caused primarily by trade imbalances. "The source of the global crisis through which we are living," he says, "can be found in the great trade and capital flow imbalances of the past decade or two." The U.S. trade policies have certainly hurt us in more ways than we immediately realize.

In the auto industry, union officials and other lobbyists are running an incessant campaign to keep automotive manufacturing jobs in the U.S. Perhaps if U.S. companies weren't taxed so heavily on their necessary components, they would be more apt to hire domestic auto workers without any union pressure whatsoever. As it is, they are pressured into hiring domestic workers, and therefore must pay the tariffs on the components they purchase internationally in order to be assembled in the United States.

The automotive industry may serve as a warning of what's to come for other manufacturing industries in which U.S. companies operate. Political pressure is always on business decision makers to employ domestic workers to assemble products. Yet, our trade policy penalizes them for doing so. This catch-22 American executives face is one of the primary reasons why American manufacturing companies are finding it so difficult to be competitive with other countries in the global economy.

If American manufacturing is to be revived, a new trade policy will have to play a critical role. American business executives must exercise what influence they have to make changes in the U.S. trade policy—changes that bolster the manufacturing industry and serve the U.S. economy within the context of free global trade.

This is reason number two why our organizations are dysfunctional.

CHAPTER 3:
THE WALMARTING OF AMERICA

The Dysfunctional Organization

Chapter 3

"Save Money. Live Better." At the time of this writing, that is Walmart's mantra. It's in the commercials. It's on the website. It's on the delivery trucks. Walmart prides itself on selling low-priced items to free up the budgets of its customers. Indeed, some variation of that statement has always been its *modus operandi*. Walmart has always been about low prices. This is why Americans love Walmart.

Sam Walton was an American icon. A cheerleader, entrepreneur and a solid visionary. The concept of expanding on the original five and dime model of F.W. Woolworth and S.S. Kresge was no doubt ingenious. Sam took it one step further by reaching out to folks in rural America that were forgotten by the mass merchandisers. Yes, Sears, Roebuck & Company were in a number of small towns with catalogue order stores, but no one gave customers personal attention like Sam Walton. Sam was a retail genius.

In his autobiography, *Made in America*, Walton (1993) says, "So we know what we have to do: keep lowering our prices, keep improving our service, and keep making things better for the folks who shop in our stores. That is not something we can simply do in a general way. It isn't something we can command from the executive offices because we want it to happen. We have to do it store by store, department by department, customer by customer, associate by associate." What can be wrong with such an approach to business?

Let me explain a little bit about exactly what I mean about the Walmarting of America. First, Walmart is a great American success story. It serves a need in the marketplace by giving people what they want at the lowest prices around. And being the free market economist that I am, I sure do admire what Walmart has done. They have filled a very significant market need in America for years. They are convenient, always seemingly in a strip mall close by. They are efficient. They carry just about anything a person could want at arguably the lowest price around. Walmart is fulfilling a need that Americans have for all the reasons I stated above. However, at what cost?, and at what cost to society?

Charles Fishman (2006), author of *The Wal-Mart Effect*, sums up the Walmart pricing philosophy in this way: "Buy stuff cheap. Sell it cheap. And if you're going to sell the same stuff as every other store, but cheaper than they sell it, controlling your own costs has to be more than a goal. It has to be a fundamental element of your business every day." With such a stringent focus on cutting costs, there may be some unintended consequences for consumers.

There are citizens in certain states that have banded together to protest against Walmarts opening in their neighborhoods. They argue that Walmart destroys their choice of retailers and puts the little guy out of business. Being the free market economist that I am, I say, "You want Walmart, Americans, you got Walmart."

But it cuts deeper than that. Years ago I was working in the motor business and watching the meteoric rise of Royal Appliance out of Cleveland, Ohio. You see, Royal was a sleepy, well-respected organization that only made high end floor care products, until they came up with the concept called "The Dirt Devil." The Dirt Devil was a revolutionary hand held vacuum that was good for your camper, cabin, garage, and all those little messes the kids make at home when the parents aren't watching.

I worked on the original design. It was sleek and all plastic. It was lightweight and it was cool. And most importantly, it was red, just like the devil. This product sent Royal stock soaring and it became the darling of the community of Cleveland. Royal began looking for more ways to increase their market penetration, so they developed upright vacuum cleaners. Obviously, these guys understood marketing, because they were manufacturing red plastic Dirt Devils. Remember, at the time, all of the vacuum cleaners in the marketplace were pretty mundane. This product of theirs' would catch anyone's eye at the retailer, with the color and then the name.

At the time, Walmart was on this buy local kick and soon K-Mart followed. I can remember being in their stores, and above the check outs were a list of all the local vendors and local brands you could find in their store. That all changed in the mid-nineties, however, and just why did it change? American consumer tastes were changing and so was Walmart's advertising. Now appearing every twenty minutes on your television screen was the little smiley face from Walmart with his sword, slashing prices. You see, Walmart was becoming synonymous with low pricing strategy. And today, when you get behind a Walmart truck on the freeway, the slogan still reads, "Lowest Prices Always".

Well, Royal Appliance got caught up in the Walmart dilemma. In order for them to be a meaningful brand they had to have shelf space at Walmart. As a smart retailer, Walmart gave the best shelf space to the brand that could generate the most sales activity, and as Royal's competitors caught up with it, they were forced to chase low-cost labor dollars around the world. Royal had to go back to their suppliers for resins, plastic housings, brushes bags and ask for price reductions. That forced these suppliers to scour the world for lower cost components so they could still make some money. That shifted jobs from the US to Asia. It wasn't long after that that we were chasing lower assembly jobs for the entire product and we were manufacturing the entire cleaner in Asia.

This has happened in more than one industry. It doesn't take much to figure out that we have lost our ability to manufacture in this nation. The New England area used to be the watchmaking capital of the world. The spring industry sprung (pardon my pun) out of the watch making industry, because needs drive innovation. The south was full of textile plants, the Midwest and New England were full of shoe manufacturers and woolen mills, there was steel in Pittsburgh and the Mahoning Valley of Ohio, rubber products and tires in Akron, glass in Toledo, and (the dilemma we are facing currently) automobiles from Detroit.

My point is simple. America is steadily losing any industry of its own. We are becoming a reseller of the world's goods. We, as the largest consuming society in the world, expect to pay less every time we go to Walmart. Walmart knows this is what Americans want. Unfortunately for Americans, it means the loss of solid, well-paying manufacturing jobs as a consequence.

While many in the media have lambasted Walmart as the ultimate embodiment of evil corporations, that is not my intention. If it wasn't Sam Walton, it would have been someone else. The fact of the matter is that the Walmarting of America isn't something that has been done solely by Walmart. It's something that has been done by the demands of American consumers.

While being the company to set the precedent for low prices, Walmart isn't the only company doing the "Walmarting." Other major retailers, from Target to Best Buy, have initiated price matching programs to the extent that Walmart's domination in the low-price arena has become merely a matter of perception. Almost every major retailer in the U.S. has now officially been Walmarted.

When we look around the country and see a desolate landscape of abandoned factories, we are gazing upon the work of our very own hands. While the middle class is continually growing overseas, our middle glass is shrinking. Why? Because the well-paying manufacturing jobs that once defined the middle glass have disappeared during the last several decades. According to Robert Morley (2006) of online magazine *The Trumpet*, "Manufacturing as a share of the economy has been plummeting. In 1965, manufacturing accounted for 53 percent of the economy. By 1988 it only accounted for 39 percent, and in 2004, it accounted for just 9 percent."

And what has replaced those lost manufacturing jobs? Well, instead of making the products for Walmart, workers dislocated from the outsourced manufacturing jobs have been selling the products for Walmart. According to *AOL Jobs* contributor Kaitlin Madden 2010), the most common job in the U.S. today is that of a retail salesperson, at 4,209,500 workers. The second most common job in the U.S. today is that of a cashier, at 3,439,380 workers. The average annual salaries of such positions? $24,630 and $19,030, respectively. The average annual salary of a worker in manufacturing? $50,000 (*Simply Hired*, 2013).

We have brought this dilemma on ourselves. Human beings are notorious for being oblivious to unintended consequences. Perhaps we as Americans are the worst of all. We know that our iPhones are made by workers in other countries, but we want them as cheaply as we can get them. We know that our "American" automobiles are made using components sourced from across the globe, but we want them as cheaply as we can get them. Walmart didn't ship our jobs overseas. We did. When we started demanding lower prices and casting our dollar votes on those companies that could supply them, we unwittingly relinquished our jobs. Now, we're stuck scanning the barcodes of products we used to take pride in making. At least now we get a 10% employee discount.

So the question again becomes, "Where do we go from here?" Many Americans have begun taking part in various "Buy American" movements. It's a marketing message that resonates with consumers who feel nostalgic about the prosperity of the Industrial Age. The Made in America Movement (Uke, 2013) , a community of manufacturers primarily using domestically sourced materials and labor, holds with this message: "To rebuild the manufacturing greatness in this country, more needs to be made here. That isn't to say that trade is bad, or that foreign countries as a whole are to blame for our economic troubles. But we have outsourced too much of our industry, and have purchased too much from unequal trade partners."

But I dare you to try to buy American. Firstly, is your Chevrolet American? You can buy a pair of Allen-Edmonds shoes, but you cannot afford them on a retail salary (Great product, by the way and made in Port Washington, Wisconsin, but again, be prepared to pay for quality and for something being American-made), but don't look for a shirt, because the last of those factories closed. You can find pants made in the United States, but you'd better look hard and long because just a handful of companies make them now.

Another organization, The Made in USA Foundation (2012), has this to say: "Support U.S. jobs and the U.S. economy by buying American. When you buy a product made from China, the jobs you're supporting are the jobs of the Chinese. The more we allow industries to outsource and the more we buy foreign-made the less demand companies have to keep the American workforce healthy, happy, and busy. We need to hold ourselves accountable and make the change to buy American."

Still another organization, Made in USA Certified (2013), sells certification labels to American manufacturers that provide assurance to American consumers that the products they are purchasing are manufactured in America. One popular consumer driven website, *Keeping America at Work* (2013), uses the slogan, "We are not out of work because the economy is bad. The economy is bad because we are out of work." Clearly, there is at least an undercurrent in American consumer culture that demands a return of manufacturing to the United States.

American companies who ship jobs overseas, regardless of the financial necessities of doing so, are heavily criticized by average American citizens. On the other hand, companies that keep jobs in the U.S. are heralded as leaders. Perhaps one of the most startling and telling bits of trivia about the modern American economy is that millions of dollars' worth of American flags are imported from China each year (Flag Manufacturers Association of America, 2012). Annin, an American-based flag manufacturer that has been making American flags in Coshocton, Ohio since 1847, has repeatedly become a star of both its customers and the media. One satisfied customer Jerry Grezlik from Ohio, has this to say: "Recently I purchased one of your flags. I bought it because it was made in the USA. If it had been made in China, it would still be in the store. It is not often that a consumer has the opportunity to buy US made products. Thank you for making the flags here and keeping the jobs here." (Annin Flagmakers, 2013)

In the end, yes, it's the consumers that are going to determine whether or not manufacturing plays a role in America's future. The "maker movement," as chronicled by Chris Anderson (2012) in Makers, sheds some light on the possibility of a return to manufacturing in America with the advent of low-cost 3D printing and computer aided design. "The third industrial revolution," says Anderson, "is best seen as the combination of digital manufacturing and personal manufacturing: the industrialization of the Maker Movement."

Again, of all places, Youngstown, Ohio plays a role in the additive manufacturing strategy with 3D printing. This is taken directly from the North American Additive Manufacturing website (NAMMI):

> "Additive manufacturing, often referred to as three-dimensional (3D) printing, is a way of making products and components from a digital model, and is being applied in a wide range of industries, including defense, aerospace, automotive, medical, and metals

manufacturing. Like an office printer that puts 2D digital files on a piece of paper, a 3D printer creates components by depositing thin layers of material, one after another, using a digital blueprint until the exact component required has been created. There are many different technologies for additive manufacturing, and each one is best suited to different product applications and requirements. Some of the technologies have been used for rapid prototyping for decades, but new developments are allowing them to be used for actual production.

Key benefits of additive manufacturing are that it enables shorter lead times, mass customization, reduced parts count, more complex shapes, parts on demand, less material waste, and lower life-cycle energy use. The Department of Defense envisions customizing parts on-site for operational systems that would otherwise be expensive to make or ship. The Department of Energy anticipates that additive processes would be able to save more than 50 percent of energy use compared to today's 'subtractive' manufacturing processes."

This process could drive manufacturing in the future. If not, it sure has some tremendous implications for the healthcare market, as even tissues and muscles become printable.

That is what is great about these times we are living in. Innovation is driving us to points once believed unimaginable.

Nevertheless, managers of American manufacturing companies can still make a difference with their marketing. Just as Wal-Mart's "Save Money. Live Better." slogan appeals to some consumers, the "Buy American" slogan appeals to other consumers. By encouraging consumers to make investments in American-made products, companies may yet again encourage growth in the manufacturing sector of the American economy.

This is reason number three why our organizations are dysfunctional.

The Dysfunctional Organization

CHAPTER 4:
THE LABOR MISPERCEPTION

The Dysfunctional Organization

Chapter 4

In his classic work on labor, *Human Capital*, Nobel Prize winning economist Gary Becker (1994) introduces the thin line between labor and capital. "If capital exploits labor," he asks, "does human capital exploit labor too--in other words, do some workers exploit other workers? And are skilled workers and unskilled workers pitted against each other in the alleged class conflict between labor and capital? If governments are to expropriate all capital to end such conflict, should they also expropriate human capital, so that government would take over ownership of workers as well?"

One of the most damaging beliefs among executives in the U.S. today is the high cost of labor. Workers are too expensive, so we ship their jobs to lower wage workers overseas. That is the story we've been told. The media always has a field day when jobs are outsourced, and keeping jobs in America is the platform of many a political candidate. "Buying American," as already mentioned, is a hot consumer trend these days. All around us, we are bombarded with messaging reinforcing our beliefs that workers in the U.S. are just too expensive and, if we want to survive, we have to find lower wage workers in countries outside of the United States.

Seriously though, think about the cost of labor. What is the cost of labor involved in, say, die casting? Historically, it has been high, but think about it in its optimal sense. I had a good friend in the die-casting business, and the high cost of labor drove him out of business. "Why?" you might ask.

Well, it helps if you know something about the process. Hot aluminum is injected into a die and cured, and it ejects a die casting. Die castings are used in many automotive applications, from motors all the way to door handles. My friend did business the traditional way. He had a die department, a casting area, a furnace, or melting, department, and a trimming, or secondary, operation. Can you imagine how much indirect labor he had moving parts around his shop, let alone shrinkage? Parts would be in queue around his shop waiting for the next operation to be performed. Now the smart way to do this is:

1) Have the dies located near the press in which they run.
2) Have them ready to stage into the press.
3) Have the ladle as close to the press as possible.

4) Mold the part.

5) Trim the part at the press.

6) Do any secondary at the press.

7) Put it into the box for the customer.

Now what have we eliminated by doing this? Well, we have one labor operation complete the part instead of five or six. We eliminate the need for indirect labor. We minimize spoilage and we respond much quicker to our customers' needs. My friend is out of business. He says its due to the high cost of labor. I say it is because of the high cost of management. Who designed his processes? This was the way it was done since the fifties, when his dad started the business. Labor did not put him out of business, he put himself out of business because he could not react to competition. It is usually our unwillingness to accept change and reevaluate our processes that causes us to fail. Our labor costs are not too high.

Is process reengineering the answer? "Business process reengineering (BPR) is the analysis and redesign of workflow within and between enterprises. BPR reached its heyday in the early 1990's when Michael Hammer and James Champy published their best-selling book, *Reengineering the Corporation*. The authors promoted the idea that sometimes radical redesign and reorganization of an enterprise (wiping the slate clean) is necessary to lower costs and increase quality of service, and that information technology is the key enabler for that radical change.

Hammer and Champy felt that the design of workflow in most large corporations was based on assumptions about technology, people, and organizational goals that are no longer valid. They suggested seven principles of reengineering to streamline the work process and thereby achieve significant levels of improvement in quality, time management, and cost:

1. Organize around outcomes, not tasks.
2. Identify all the processes in an organization and prioritize them in order of redesign urgency.
3. Integrate information processing work into the real work that produces the information.
4. Treat geographically dispersed resources as though they were centralized.
5. Link parallel activities in the workflow instead of just integrating their results.
6. Put the decision point where the work is performed, and build control into the process.
7. Capture information once—at the source.

By the mid-nineties, BPR gained the reputation of being a nice way of saying "downsizing." According to Hammer, lack of sustained management commitment and leadership, unrealistic scope and expectations and resistance to change prompted management to abandon the concept of BPR and embrace the next new methodology, enterprise resource planning (ERP).' This definition was posted by Margaret Rouse on Search CIO in 2009.

I have to add that in all practicality, it is much more than that. If you take it one step further, you'll realize that everything in life is a process and can be mapped as such. By that standard, isn't everything we do in manufacturing a process? So, if we look at eliminating waste and creating a streamlined process, we can overshadow the cost of labor in every way.

Creating efficiencies is what started the "lean revolution," and today this concept has gone from the manufacturing floor to the operating room and patient care, because we can now give patients entire holistic treatments and services, while expediting their return to health as well.

Who was the largest net exporter of goods in the world in 2011? I expect you to tell me China, but no.

It was Germany. What have the Germans figured out that we haven't? Well, they make sharp cars that are known for engineering and quality; they focus on high dollar, value added goods that people are willing to pay a premium for; they have skilled trades that are unmatched in the world, they have automated the everything they possibly can out of what they manufacture so that it is of world class efficiency; they educate their young in skills such as tool and die making, automation, and computer aided design so that they stay on top. Maybe we can learn a lesson from the Germans.

Many managers operate under the assumption that expensive labor is the main reason why costs are high, and that the only way to survive is to outsource jobs to lower cost workers overseas. This can sometimes be the case. But I am going to argue that the cost of labor in the U.S. is greatly exaggerated and that it is a red herring, distracting managers from the real issue--themselves.

In *The Practice of Management*, Peter Drucker (2006) explains the rise of the professional employee what has come to be known as skilled labor. "In addition to the physicists who have entered industry so spectacularly during these last ten years, businesses today are employing thousands of geologists, biologists, and other natural scientists, and at least hundreds of economists, statisticians, certified public accountants and psychologists—not to mention lawyers." Drucker goes on to surmise that technology will only increase the amount of skilled labor necessary to operate the business.

Labor is not the problem. Management is the problem. Management often inanely constructs policies that unnecessarily add to costs. In the sixties, at Youngstown Sheet and Tube, management crafted a policy that gave workers 13 weeks of vacation. Workers never asked for it. The union leadership had asked for it and executives simply allowed it. Of course labor costs are going to be high when you pay workers for three months that they aren't producing anything, and most organized labor would likely agree.

Sadly, policies like this are still around in many U.S. manufacturing companies. Workers are allowed extensive time off—time they don't even ask for. Workers are given pensions and benefits that they don't want or even fully understand. But, because of archaic company and human resource policies, managers add these costs to labor. Workers don't often realize how much they cost employers. Most of the time, workers don't even know many of the costs

that managers are arbitrarily adding to keeping them
employed.

But the poor allocation of resources by managers
is only half of the reason why labor costs are high.
There is a much more important and much more
prevalent issue in managing labor costs in the U.S.
Why are labor costs always seemingly so high? It isn't
the workers. It is management's inefficient allocation
of labor and capital. It isn't that cheaper workers are
needed. Often, it is that we are having men doing the
work that should be done by machines.

You can only chase the outsourcing model so far.
Eventually, you are going to run out of countries to
ship jobs to. Once we outsource to the Congo, I
don't quite know where we can exploit labor again.
Eventually, the labor costs in other countries are
going to rise. You will always be chasing a cheaper
workforce, always moving your operations from one
place to another. Where are you going to go next—
Vietnam? Africa? It's always going to be changing.
Why not instead eliminate the jobs that don't need
human beings, and allow machines to do the
mundane work? Give jobs to higher skilled workers
who deserve the high wages you pay them.
Automation is one of the only ways to keep your
business alive and keep good jobs in the U.S.

But who makes the decision to automate? It isn't the workers. It's the management team. The problem with most manufacturing decision makers today is they get their people and processes mixed up. Most manufacturing executives in America build their systems around their people. The only way for them to run a sustainable business, including providing sustainable jobs for workers, is to build their people around their systems. What I mean is this: we operate under the notion that jobs are roles that need to be filled. Instead, we should view jobs as tasks that need to be completed.

The only way to offer competitive prices that are attractive to consumers is to properly leverage people and systems. As a consultant to industry, I continually use the phrase, "People, process, and technology." Those three words are key in solving most problems. Proper systems should always be in place before considering how people function in them. All too often, though, managers simply put people to work and allow the system to arise organically. The result is often that workers do redundant tasks, or that entire roles are created that are unnecessary to get a project finished.

That is where automation and technology comes in. If the proper systems are in place prior to finding people to perform tasks, automation will be the default. If a task needs to be completed, we should always ask first, "Can this task be automated?" We should always consider first whether or not the job can be performed by a machine. If the answer is no, then and only then should we add workers.

The result is that workers will then be added who have more secure futures, because their skills are actually in demand. And yes, at first, there will be fewer workers. But as the business grows through increased efficiency, more workers will be added. Only this time, these workers will actually be skilled enough to maintain their jobs.

It is a large stretch to blame workers for high costs of labor. They are just doing what they're told. In order for American companies to regain their previous success, managers will have to take responsibility for their misallocation of resources. Managers will have to look at their businesses with new eyes, with systems considered first and people considered second.

Entrepreneurship expert Michael Gerber (1990), in his respected work *The E-Myth Revisited*, makes the claim that businesses should hire people with as little skill as possible. "If yours is a legal firm, you must have attorneys," says Gerber. "If yours is a medical firm, you must have physicians. But you don't need to hire brilliant attorneys or brilliant physicians. You need to create the very best system through which good attorneys and good physicians can be leveraged to produce exquisite results. The question you need to keep asking yourself is: how can I give my customer the results he wants systematically rather than personally?"

Again, this does not mean that people aren't important. It simply means that, if we are to give workers jobs that are actually sustainable and in demand, we must allow automation to perform lower skill tasks that would not be stable sources of income for workers in ever-growing, technologically-advanced societies. If we want to be competitive and keep good jobs in our country, we must be willing to be smarter with our resources. The future is coming, whether we like it or not. The only question for U.S. companies is this: are we going to be riding the wave or are we going to drown beneath it?

In an article for the *MIT Technology Review*, columnist David Rotman (2013) cites research from MIT's Sloan School of Management, suggesting that an increase in technological efficiency is coming, at the expense of destroying more and more jobs:

That robots, automation, and software can
replace people might seem obvious to anyone
who's worked in automotive manufacturing
or as a travel agent. But Brynjolfsson and
McAfee's claim is more troubling and
controversial. They believe that rapid
technological change has been destroying jobs
faster than it is creating them, contributing to
the stagnation of median income and the
growth of inequality in the United States.
And, they suspect, something similar is
happening in other technologically advanced
countries.

In other words, the speed at which technology is
increasing seems to be exceeding the speed at which
people can find new roles in the workforce.
Throughout history, there have always been displaced
workers during technological revolutions, but today,
the technology is just moving too quickly for people
to adapt.

What does this mean for manufacturing—or any
business for that matter? Does management have an
obligation to maintain a certain number of flesh-and-
blood workers, regardless of its impact on
productivity? In their modern classic *The End of*

The Dysfunctional Organization

Prosperity, authors Arthur Laffer (2008) and Peter
Tanous remind us of a story often attributed to
Milton Friedman. The authors write: "Our friend the
late Milton Friedman once told us a story of being in
India in the 1960s and watching thousands of workers
build a canal with shovels. Milton asked the lead
engineer, Why don't you have tractors to help build
this canal? The engineer replied, 'You don't
understand, Mr. Friedman, this canal is a jobs
program to provide work for as many men as
possible.' Milton responded with his classic wit, 'Oh, I
see. I thought you were trying to build a canal. If you
really want to create jobs, then by all means give these
men spoons, not shovels.'"

Do contemporary revolutions in technology pose
a difficult problem for maintaining an optimum level
of employment in society? Absolutely. I would argue
that it is a good problem to have, but I will concede
that it is a problem. But, from the vantage point of
business leaders, it is a distraction from the main
purpose of the enterprise. As in Milton Friedman's
story, you, as a business leader, need to ask yourself
what the purpose of your company is. Is it to build
canals or to create jobs? If, as I suspect, it is the
former, then I would argue that your primary
obligation to both your shareholders and society is to

use what technology is available to you to build canals. Let us worry about finding new jobs. Chances are, we'll need your canals to get them.

This is reason number four why our organizations are dysfunctional.

CHAPTER 5:
THE LOSS OF INDIVIDUALISM
AND
THE AGE OF GENERIC
MANAGEMENT

The Dysfunctional Organization

Chapter 5

In 1911, when Frederick Winslow Taylor published his book, *Principles of Scientific Management*, we were in the heart of the industrial revolution. Business leaders of the time welcomed this type of empirical research. It made their operations more efficient, providing tasks that were interchangeable among workers. It also made their operations more efficient, providing consistent, repeatable routines for each worker to perform. Ultimately, it made their businesses more scalable—as mass production became possible with low-skill labor and efficient processes.

I have no problem with scientific management. Using its principles helped to strengthen the processes that built many of our country's most successful, even legendary, organizations. However, over a century later, I think that scientific management has begun to do more harm than good. Somewhere along the line, the man became subservient to the machine. Somewhere along the line, those controlling the process became slaves to the process. Somewhere along the line, innovation was replaced by the time-honored tradition of the status quo.

Live Science (2013) says,

> You may have heard people describe themselves as strictly "right-brained" or "left-brained," with the left-brainers bragging about their math skills and the right-brainers touting their creativity.

That's because the brain is divided down the middle into two hemispheres, with each half performing a fairly distinct set of operations. Much of what is known about brain function is owed to Roger Sperry, whose experiments examined the way the human brain's hemispheres operate both independently and in concert with each other. The two hemispheres communicate information, such as sensory observations, to each other through the thick corpus callosum that connects them.

The brain's right hemisphere controls the muscles on the left side of the body, while the left hemisphere controls the muscles on the right side of the human body. When you wink your right eye, that's the left side of your brain at work. Because of this criss-crossed wiring, damage to one side of the brain affects the opposite side of the body.

In general, the left hemisphere is dominant in language: processing what you hear and handling most of the duties of speaking. It's also in charge of carrying out logic and exact mathematical computations. When you need to retrieve a fact, your left brain pulls it from your memory.

The right hemisphere is mainly in charge of spatial abilities, face recognition and processing music. It performs some math, but only rough estimations and comparisons. The brain's right side also helps us to comprehend visual imagery and make sense of what we see. It plays a role in language, particularly in interpreting context and a person's tone. As for whether a person is right-brained or left-brained, or even right-handed or left-handed the uses and preferences of the brain's two sections are far more complex than just a simple left vs. right equation. For example, some people throw a ball with their right hand but write with their left.

Whether it is a matter of right brain/left brain or whether it is a matter of lack of creativity in the organization can be described in the approaches involving several disciplines: psychology, cognitive science, education, philosophy (particularly the philosophy of science), technology, theology, sociology, linguistics, business studies, songwriting and economics, taking in the relationship between creativity and general intelligence, mental and neurological processes associated with creativity, the relationships between personality type and creative ability and between creativity and mental health, the potential for fostering creativity through education and training, especially as augmented by technology, and the application of creative resources to improve the effectiveness of learning and teaching processes.

It seems like the only industry in which innovation remains a powerful motive force is the tech industry, manifested in Silicon Valley. In his thorough account of the history of Google, technology writer Steven Levy (2011) explains how an innovative and creative workforce is the top priority at Google. Levy writes about the "Googliness" requirement the company has for hiring its people. Being smart is a given but, beyond that, candidates must also possess a creative intuition that fits with the company's culture. As such, the interviews are loaded with brain teasers, games, and sometimes outlandish problem-solving activities.

An article for Forbes (He, 2013) further explains how 'Google empowers its employees to do more creative work. Google allows direct access from its employees to its top leaders, provides cafes across the campus that build community and foster collaboration, and hosts weekly all-hands-on-deck meetings in which issues are raised and resolved with top management. Most notably, though, Google offers its famous "20% time," in which employees are given 20% of their time to work on their own creative projects. Some of Google's most valuable products, including GMail, have emerged from this creative work."

You see, at least the early entrepreneurs of the industrial revolution were innovative risk takers, seizing opportunities instead of following orders. These early titans of industry changed the game by breaking the rules and changing the norms. More and more, though, the leaders who are graduating from our business schools and reading from our business books are taught that the way to climb the corporate ladders is to follow rules—not to break them. More and more, innovation is losing out to bureaucracy.

Recently, the Institute for Corporate Productivity published a study surveying some of the top companies and people in the fields of management and innovation. They examined some of the best people management practices at organizations known for innovation and found several ways that those companies develop and manage their human capital. In summarizing their findings, here are 10 human capital practices that drive innovation:

- **Use Technology to Collaborate and Share Knowledge**. Collaboration drives creativity and innovation, and social media and conferencing technologies can help bring people together (or virtually together) more often for that collaboration.

- **Promote Innovation as an Organizational Value**. The most innovative companies didn't just luck into hiring creative people; they placed creative and even average people into creative cultures.

- **Include Innovation as a Leadership Development Competency**. Part of building an innovative culture is having leaders who value creativity, and who are creative themselves.

- **Tie Compensation to Innovation**. The jury is still deliberating the influence of incentives on creativity, but their use in organizations sends a signal that innovation is valued. That signal is an important part of culture building.

- **Develop an "Idea-finding" Program**. As we've discussed elsewhere, it's not enough to have great ideas. Innovative companies build a system that taps into the collective knowledge of everyone and lets everyone promote good ideas.

- **Fund Outside Projects**. It might sound counterintuitive to allow funding to develop projects that are technically outside your organization, but as market boundaries continue to blur, strategic innovation partnerships become even more important.

- **Train for Creativity**. Creativity isn't innate. Creative thinking skills can be developed, and the most innovative companies fund training programs to develop them.

- **Create a Review Process for Innovative Ideas**. Even the best ideas don't come fully formed. There is a process to refining, developing and identifying the ideas with the most market potential. Creating a review process allows this to happen and signals that innovative ideas are valued.

- **Recruit for Creative Talent**. Especially at the undergraduate and graduate levels. The war for talent is slowing shifting its focus from quantitative minds to creative ones.

- **Reward Innovation with Engaging Work.** Research demonstrates that companies that are able to identify their most creative employees can enhance their creative ability by providing them autonomy to work on projects that are naturally interesting to them.

In most modern organizations, conformity is rewarded and innovation is stymied. Leaders aren't looking to inspire their workers to find creative solutions to business problems; instead, they are looking to enforce rules upon the workers. The problem is that the nature of work has changed. The portion of the workforce that needed to be controlled has largely been replaced by machines. We need workers today that are capable of thinking outside of the box, but we are trying to treat those workers like they are on assembly lines. We are trying to automate creativity.

As Daniel Pink describes in *A Whole New Mind* (2006), "In an age of abundance, appealing only to rational, logical, and functional needs is woefully insufficient. Engineers must figure out how to get things to work. But if those things are not also pleasing to the eye or compelling to the soul, few will buy them. There are too many other options." He goes on to say that, "Mastery of design, empathy, play, and other seemingly soft aptitudes are now the main way for individuals and firms to stand out in a crowded marketplace."

We have traded inspirational leadership for canned leadership, which is in fact no leadership at all. The leaders of the modern organization are simply regurgitating the business knowledge of the past that they were spoon fed all the way into their positions of leadership. Even the leaders themselves are slaves to the rules—the rules of yesterday's status quo. They won't allow their workers the freedom to take risks, but nor will they take those risks themselves. And this is the heart of the problem—no one is allowed to take risks.

Risk is neither a good thing nor a bad thing; it is simply a reality. And, of course, not every business decision should be risky. We should never take risks simply for the sake of being risky. However, every business decision should be made with the willingness to take risks. That's what we've lost in our organizations today—the willingness. Nobody is willing. Our workers aren't willing, because they know you won't like it and they will lose their jobs. We, as leaders, aren't willing, because we don't want to look like idiots if it doesn't work. So, we stay where we are—stagnant, but comfortable all the same.

Thinking outside of the box is cliché, but that's exactly what we need to do. Or, at the very least, we should be empowering our employees to do it. How can we expect to think outside of the box when we won't even allow our employees the freedom of imagining what it looks like outside of the box? Before we are capable of thinking outside of the box, we must leave the box. We must embrace the willingness to disrupt the current way of doing things. We must defy tradition. We must look at benchmarks that show how we compare to other companies in our industries, and then do something so wildly different that we carve out an entirely new industry.

Our employees would be more than willing to try out new things if we would simply give them that freedom. But they're scared. It's almost as if we have a sign on our doors when we hire them, which says, "No New Ideas Welcome Here." We've taught our employees that asking questions is a bad thing. We have destroyed their curiosity. We've created a workforce that is terrified to even ask for permission to take on a new project. What we need is a workforce that takes the initiative to launch new projects and then asks not for our permission, but rather for our reaction.

A large part of the problem is that employees don't really believe in the work they are doing for their company. Even leaders don't believe in their companies anymore. All too often, leaders and workers alike are guns for hire. They're just looking for the next best opportunity and will jump ship as soon as someone else offers it. The problem with this system is that it creates a bureaucracy in the modern organization. No one is working for the customer, or working to change the industry, or working to make the world a better place. Everyone is working for his boss. The boss is the number one customer. That's the culture we've created.

The Dysfunctional Organization

In his work on leadership, *Start with Why*, author Simon Sinek (2011) explains how leaders use a sense of purpose to inspire their followers to take action. Rather than giving the "I have a plan" speech, Martin Luther King gave the "I have a dream" speech. In other words, King liberated his followers to take action and resolve the racial issues of the time in their own way. "Leaders are people in power positions," says Sinek. "Those who lead, inspire us, whether they are individuals or they are organizations, we follow those who lead, not because we have to, but because we want to."

But what if we changed things? What if we taught our employees, when taking on new projects to ask not, "Will this be okay with my boss?" but instead, "Will this be okay with my customer?" Think about how that would change our businesses. What if we tore down those innovation-stifling signs that limit our creativity we have hanging on our doors as new employees enter our businesses and replaced them with signs that read, "New Ideas Expected Here?"

How do we evaluate our employees' work? Think about your last performance evaluation. By what standards did you judge whether or not the employee deserved a raise? Too many organizations reward employees for doing nothing. We are rewarding conformity.

Let me give you an example. On one of my performance evaluations in a previous job, I got a call from the Director in HR telling me, " I don't know what you are doing up there, but whatever it is keep doing it."

That is because I got a 95 on my leadership survey. This is a 360 degree measurement (which means you have feedback from your entire sphere of contacts) so it is important and meaningful. The department got a 55, and my boss got a 13. Probably a reason for him to get promoted. That being said, when he asked me to address how I was going to put a corrective action into HR on how I would gain my other five points I said "Why don't I help you figure out how you are going to get your other 87 points?" Needless to say, months later I was fired, and they rewarded his mediocrity. That is, they look at the employee's work and, as long as the employee hasn't done anything wrong, that employee gets a raise.

Congratulations on another year following the rules. It should be the other way around, shouldn't it? Employees should be rewarded, not for compliance, but rather for creativity. We should be asking our employees, "What have you done throughout the year that adds value to the organization?" Note: following the same rules year in and year out does not add value to the organization.

We are at a crossroads in American business. In competing economies, individuality is on the rise. Workers in emerging economies are being given freedoms to experiment and excel that they've never had before. Why are we in America beating our workers into submission? We have an amazingly broad pool of talented, creative thinkers. Why are we not using them?

The future of American business will depend on almost exclusively on our willingness—our willingness to embrace risk, our willingness to empower our creative employees, and our willingness to shift from canned leadership to the inspirational leadership that our organizations need to lead America back to a competitive stance in the global economy.

This is reason number five why our organizations are dysfunctional.

CHAPTER 6:
WHERE HAVE ALL THE LEADERS GONE?

The Dysfunctional Organization

Chapter 6

When I do my little bit on leadership versus management in my MBA class I always describe it this way, "To lead is to inspire, to manage is to control." Years ago, while teaching an undergrad class, I contrasted Warren Bennis with Peter Drucker, the world's foremost authorities on Leadership and Management. It must have been a treat for the students because I received applause at the end of my lecture. Maybe another way to put it is, leaders have followers and managers have subordinates. Leadership skills can be taught, but true leaders are born. Management skills can be taught but good managers are made. Almost everyone wants or perceives themselves to be leaders, but it doesn't happen that way. In fact, out of the masses of people I have met in my life, very few of them have been leaders.

During a trip to South Africa I hooked up with a good British/South African friend and I asked him, "Where have all the statesmen gone?" As an American, immediately Roosevelt, Kennedy, Churchill all come to mind as examples of great statesmen, and to a lesser extent, Clinton, Thatcher, Reagan, and Blair as well. It seems like whatever qualities we associated with leadership are not so prevalent today as much as yesterday, but maybe while Churchill and Roosevelt were going about their daily tasks of keeping their nations meaningful, they weren't perceived as leaders or statesmen either. Maybe history gives us that perspective. Being that we were in South Africa, I mentioned Nelson Mandela as well as F.W. DeKlerk. My friend said to me, "Wouldn't it be great if we could have dinner with Mandela?" I said of course, but that I would rather have dinner with DeKlerk. He seemed rather surprised, so I told him that we all can understand Mandela's rise to beloved status and greatness, but can we understand DeKlerk's acceptance of what was right for South Africa?

That was a little different perspective, I suppose, but we could learn as much from the guy who gave up power as well as the one who gained it. Maybe, we are on to something here as it relates to leaders and leadership. Maybe there are specific traits of a person that prove him or her as a leader—in good times, the wins, and in bad, the losses. Maybe sometimes you win and sometimes you lose, but if you always do what you think is right, will you ever have any regrets? Can you use the term statesman and leader interchangeably? Are most statesmen good leaders, and can a leader become a statesman?

Lee Iacocca (2007), famous for building the Chrysler corporation to its highest pinnacle, has recently released a sort of business memoir called, *Where Have All the Leaders Gone?* In the opening chapter, Iacocca asks, "Where are the voices of leaders who can inspire us to action and make us stand taller? What happened to the strong and resolute party of Lincoln? What happened to the courageous and populist party of FDR and Truman? There was a time in this country when the voices of great leaders lifted us up and made us want to do better. Where have all the leaders gone?" I am assuming that all leaders and statesmen have asked themselves this question.

In this chapter, I want to ask that same question. Where have all the leaders gone in the American corporation? Where are the Iacoccas? Where are the leaders who aren't afraid to push boundaries and explore in new directions?

All of the problems mentioned thus far are but symptoms of the real issue. The entrepreneurial spark has left the corporate culture in America. Leaders are leaders in name only. They don't inspire their people.

As a result, bureaucracy becomes the norm and innovation gets stifled. If the Unites States is going to become competitive again on the world's stage, it's going to do so through its executives regaining the ability to demonstrate competent leadership. One thing I always do in my management classes is to get the students to understand the difference between management and leadership. The simplest way I can put it is to say a manager controls and a leader inspires. Now, keep in mind that I am a big believer in inspirational thinking, but I am not trying to make everyone a leader—an organization can't be filled with leaders, because it is doomed if it can't manage or control like I mentioned above.

It's funny that we have always had a discussion that centers around the question of whether leaders are born or whether they can be made. Various companies have asked me for leadership training, and I have often told them that everyone does not need leadership training, and I would be careful about giving broad-based leadership training. Now keep in mind, everyone should know the difference between leaders and managers, and all should know who can be a leader and who is capable of managing a business.

In a guide for the Wall Street Journal, small business columnist Colleen Debaise (2009) paints a picture of what it means to be a leader, versus what it means to be a manager:

- The manager administers; the leader innovates.
- The manager is a copy; the leader is an original.
- The manager maintains; the leader develops.
- The manager focuses on systems and structure; the leader focuses on people.
- The manager relies on control; the leader inspires trust.
- The manager has a short-range view; the leader has a long-range perspective.
- The manager asks how and when; the leader asks what and why.
- The manager has his or her eye on the bottom line; the leader's eye is on the horizon.
- The manager imitates; the leader originates.
- The manager accepts the status quo; the leader challenges it.
- The manager is the classic good soldier; the leader is his or her own person.

- The manager does things right; the leader does the right things.

As mentioned above, leadership is about inspiring, managing is about controlling. Part of the problem with leadership among executives is that it gets confused with management. Executives at the top of organizations feel as if they need to be great managers. As a result, everyone in the organization merely conforms and does what they're told. No one is encouraged to find creative solutions to pressing problems. Therefore, there is no deviation from the status quo and, consequently, no growth. How many organizations have you known that, when the CEO reads a new book, he or she has to share it amongst their staff? Are you more inspired when this happens or less inspired? In most cases I am less inspired.

The funnel needs to be flipped. Leadership, not management, should be present at the top. Executives need to inspire the managers beneath them to be innovative and move the organization forward. It is only the people at the very bottom who need to be managed. The further down in an organization an employee is, the more he or she will need to be controlled. You'll expect your front line workers, for the most part, to follow the systems you've set in place without question. The further up in the organization an employee is, however, the more freedom he or she will need to make decisions that may have a direct influence on the company's performance.

Creativity is impossible without autonomy, but executives in organizations today don't give their managers the authority to make changes and move the company forward. What these executives should be doing is not only giving them authority, but also giving them encouragement. Essentially, executives need to become better leaders. They need to inspire their employees to take the necessary risks to create a better future for the company.

A recent move by Toyota paints a perfect picture of how corporations are giving more autonomy to their workers. Writing for the Los Angeles Times, Jerry Hirsch (2013) reports that Toyota is relinquishing control over day-to-day operations to plants in its various divisions. Hirsche quotes Toyota's president Akio Toyoda as saying, "Of course, as president, management responsibility ultimately lies with me. However, as for daily operations, we plan to implement a more agile and autonomous business unit type of structure that will enable the executive vice presidents in charge to accelerate decision-making."

What about trust? You see, my belief is that leaders have an inherent sense of trust in dealing with other individuals, but managers, well, they are quite another story. They are afraid of blackmail, fraud, and the next guy using them to jump ahead by using information to his/her advantage. That is why it is dangerous to have a manager in charge of the organization. Because of those suspicions and tendencies to distrust, imagine how ineffective it is when the distrust emanates directly from the top. You might say, that doesn't happen, but it happens often enough to keep consultants like myself busy for a long while. These are difficult organizations to fix. Most often the situation requires the removal of the CEO. Think how difficult it is to tell the CEO that he or she is the one who must move on. Organizations that do not address that issue never become healthy again. It is like a cancer festering within an organization that goes untreated until it is too late to fix. The organization gets units pared off of it and closed, or sold, or in many cases, has to file for bankruptcy.

In today's organization, there is far too much emphasis on the need to conform. As executives, our managers are too worried about meeting expectations to bother with exceeding them. They're worried about meeting quarterly results rather than focusing on growing their businesses. They're just trying to conform. And it's no surprise. We are demanding conformity. We expect them to do what they're told and threaten them when they step out of line.

Our stringent, bureaucratic rules have led us to an outbreak of organizational incest. Groupthink pervades our corporate cultures, and we punish those who think differently. There are no new ideas. There is only complacency.

This mindset is counterproductive to business success. In his groundbreaking book, *The Wisdom of Crowds*, author James Surowiecki (2005) states, "When the pressure to conform is at work, a person changes his opinion not because he actually believes something, but because it's easier to change his opinion than to challenge the group." Surowiecki goes on to tell the story of classic social experiment from Solomon Asch. In this experiment, Asch assembles a group of people—one of which is the subject of the experiment and the rest of which are, unbeknownst to the subject, accomplices of Asch. In the experiment, all of the participants look at a card and are asked to say out loud which of four lines is longer than all of the others. All of Asch's accomplices intentionally give what is clearly the wrong answer. The subject, the last person in line, then gives the wrong answer because he or she feels that, if everyone else said it was right, then it must be right. "Allowing individuals," Surowiecki says later in his book, "to pursue their own self-interest will produce collectively better results than dictating orders."

Writing for Forbes, columnist Tanya Prive (2012) offers this great list of top qualities for a successful leader:

- Honesty
- Ability to Delegate
- Communication
- Sense of Humor
- Confidence
- Commitment
- Positive Attitude
- Creativity
- Intuition
- Ability to Inspire

The one thing you most always find in a leader is his or her ability to think about you, not think about themselves. There is almost always a sense of selflessness in a great leader. The above list contains a list of qualities that I have found hold true in most cases.

What is the point of this for managers of organizations today? You want your workers to do what they do because they want to do it, not because you tell them that they have to. Why do you have to allow them that kind of freedom? Because, if you don't, then all you are going to have is a bunch of people misreading the lengths of lines because they are just following along with the herd. You don't want a team of sheep. You want a team of shepherds. You, as the leader of your organization, want to create more leaders within your organization. Because only through leadership does true innovation arise.

So, what does it take to be a leader? Here are some key morals you'll want to abide by to be an effective leader within your organization:

7 Key Attributes of a Great Leader

1. **Be sincere**. Don't act like someone's friend when you are firing them. Believe me, in one

case, my boss put his arm around my shoulder and said, "Buddy. I need to talk to you." I have never had a buddy fire me.

2. **Treat people as you would want to be treated**. Any success I have had in the world I own to two facts: I have treated people as equals, and I have never spoken down to them. Coming off as a know-it-all is a disgusting trait.

3. **Get rid of the politics**. It has no place in successful organizations. Save it for your presidential campaign, but remember that it has no place in a team setting. We should be willing to help each other because we care about the individual or ourselves and the common good of all who work with us, and arguments over politics get in the way of this.

4. **Be honest**. If someone screws up, either it's a reason to fire them or a building block for their character. Be honest with yourself when you have made a mistake and be honest with others when they have.

5.   **Trust your instincts**. If Something doesn't seem right, it probably isn't. Save your time and say no. Too many times in my career, I have made decisions that weren't exactly right, and at those times I knew it from the beginning; and boy, did it cost me.

6.   **Lead with compassion**. Put yourself in someone else's shoes. Don't act like you're compassionate, because people can see through that. Be compassionate, and if you can't be compassionate, please help the rest of us and look for another job.

7.   **Face up to your decisions**. Do your dirty work yourself. Show you have what it takes to be a leader. I call this "testicular fortitude," and it needs no explanation. If you have conviction and believe in what you are doing, please do it. I have run into many executives who hide from difficult discussions, and believe me, when this happens it highlights the fact that we have a manager in a leadership role.

Leadership is about inspiring your team. It's about encouraging them to take risks and make decisions that will build your business. It's about giving them freedom and giving them your full support in their use of it. If our organizations in the United States can once again put into places leaders who are actually willing to lead, we may have a chance of being competitive again.

This is reason number six why our organizations are dysfunctional.

CHAPTER 7:
"I CALLED TO TELL YOU YOU'RE FIRED"

The Dysfunctional Organization

<u>Chapter 7</u>

I would like to call this chapter "Balls," or "Lack of Balls," or something like that, but somehow I don't think that is politically correct. But it does make me wonder whether the phenomenon I have seen is limited to me, or whether it is prevalent in every boardroom in America. When did we lose our sense of responsibility, our sense of justice, and doing what is right because it is right? Why can't we face up to our responsibilities like humans? I have been fired a number of times in my career. Yes, I will admit I like to instigate, but when I find people with no testicular fortitude it drives me crazy, and the business world is full of them these days.

I recently stumbled across a provocative article by investor Sally Krawcheck (2013) called "The 7 Things I Learned When I Got Fired (Again)." Being fired, the thinking goes, is the absolute worst thing that could happen to a professional. And many managers today seem to operate under the belief that the biggest motivator for an employee is the fear of getting fired. Like me, Krawcheck takes a different perspective. Here is what she has learned from her experience:

If it feels too good to be true, it probably is.

- Corporate culture is everything.
- Face-to-face meeting time is important.
- Find a key mentor, sponsor, or connection within the company.
- Politics often trump business results.
- Develop a strong network outside of the company.
- Always express gratitude.

The bottom line is, there is no room for the individual in the corporation. So, does it surprise you I have been fired a few times? Not easy to figure out, is it? I have never been a conformist, and I have always spoken up for the little guys, and, well, big guys don't like that very much. It reminds me of the days when the mills were still operating in Youngstown, Ohio, and I had a uncle that was a superintendent in the mills. Well, I don't need tell you that 95% of Youngstown Ohioans are Democrats. I mean it's a mill town with a bunch of blue collar workers, so what do you expect? Strong working class people, union environment, all Democrats, right? Well as I said my uncle, he was a conformist, and since he was in management he had to be a Republican. That was the line: Management meant

Republican, Worker meant Democrat. I have never seen a bigger conformist. Since my uncle thought it would get him somewhere, and since he was management, he voted Republican. I have never been like that; I would do the opposite just to piss people off.

Anyway, back to being fired…When are these people that do the firing going to grow some balls and be men? The first time it happened I had been employed by this electric motor company for nine years. I had a series of health issues, which included some bad surgeries to repair a herniated stomach, and I had been recently diagnosed with Chronic Lymphocytic Leukemia. The organization passed me around like a baton. First I worked for the Group President, and when he saw he didn't have a yes man, he passed me off on the Division President. That guy was a puppet; a jellyfish had more of a spine than this man. Long story short, he is still there after all these years and I am writing my story.

We hired a new vice president of manufacturing and I was passed on to him. The day I shook his hand, I decided he and I weren't going to get along. One of his first actions was to move me out of my office because it was larger than his. Folks, do me one favor and do not, I repeat, do not, come in and move everyone around the office, capturing the largest piece of real estate for yourself. It is not the way to build a team. The summer went on and my relationship with him deteriorated.

The inevitable day came, and he called me in his office by standing in my doorway and saying "Hey Buddy, I need to talk to you." First of all, we both knew we weren't buddies, so why would he go with that as his way of breaking the ice? What an icebreaker. He sat and I sat, and he was scared shitless, stumbling and muttering while reading the script he had received from human resources. My first comment was, "Are you a little nervous?" which only had the effect of making him more jittery. Inside I was laughing my ass off because just two weeks before I had accepted my next position, which was in Canada, and I was just waiting for my immigration papers and work authorization to be issued. The only thing that had to be decided between us was how much money the organization was going to throw on the table, and then I walked away a happy man.

I called my wife, who, like every wife, was terrified at the prospect of a husband with a life-threatening disease and no job. She asked "Are you all right?" and I said of course. She asked "What are you

going to do the rest of the day?" and I said I was
going to play golf, and when I got home that night we
would have to go buy a car (I had lost my company
car) because we needed to do this before the bank
found out I don't have a job.

Then it was on to Canada and the electronics
industry. What a great time it was, as companies were
growing left and right, and money was being passed
around like crazy. The only problem was that I had to
work for a crazy German who was only high school
educated, but he was in his job because he had been
there twenty years. He had an ego; I mean, this guy
was a self-centered SOB. Kind of a "rags to riches
"story but undeservedly so. It was his way or no way.
Everything had to be controlled by him, lest his
superiors find out that he was a real buffoon.
Leadership skills, this guy had none. He bullied his
way around everything. His philosophy always started
with "I" or "mine." I learned a lot from this guy,
because in his mind, every modern book about
management and leadership was wrong, and only his
ideas were right. I didn't have to work for him long
but I did have interesting interactions with him.

I had been specifically recruited to help turn
around an acquisition, and it was a piece of cake, in
spite of his roadblocks. He gave me a team—the

most horrendous group of misfits, with a few potential stars (although, he wouldn't have recognized it) the folks no one in the organization wanted. As punishments to them, and trying to throw a roadblock in front of me, he gave them to me in this turnaround. Now if you wanted this turnaround to succeed, you would think you would assign your best and brightest, but not old T. He wanted to see this fail. You see, he had been forced to go outside and hire someone for this position because of an old nemesis in the organization, who had more power than old T.

Old T would have loved to see this plan fail, because then he would have one over on his old nemesis. But I wasn't about to let that happen. First of all, I took this rag tag group and made them superstars. I gave them visibility with the management, and we moved them on sight so everyone knew exactly what we were doing. Again, isn't it all about leadership and empowerment. They started to shine, and in a short while we helped that division break even. Like I said, I was there only a short time and I could see through T.

So one day I received an offer to leave that company and work somewhere else. I prepared a quarterly update for T and I went to his office to present it. He berated me about my style of management and told me it really didn't fit with the organization, as only the style of a true imbecile like old T could fit. Like I said, I had an offer in my pocket, so I prepared my resignation. Once I sat with T and told him the news, his face flushed and he looked at me with this blank stare. I waved my hand in front of him and said I was preparing to leave. His first response was "You can't go…" I asked, "Why would you want me here when last week you basically told me I was incompetent." He said, "I didn't mean that." To which I replied, "Do you have a habit of saying things you don't mean? Are you crazy?"

Anyway, I caught T at a bad time because he was on his way to Europe, and he asked me to keep my phone on over the weekend. I immediately shut it off and let him stew on our discussion for the next few days. I am nothing, if I am not strategically stubborn. Long story short, I got what I wanted—I stayed with the company and had a five year run. But old T gets the award for incompetent management. You see, leaders are concerned about you, managers are concerned about results, and nincompoops like old T are concerned about themselves. How they stay employed and fly under the radar is beyond me.

My new situation wasn't without problems, though. When I got there I met P and I came into the organization higher than he did. The company paid for my housing and expenses, while P got nothing. We, in fact, had to share an office for a while. I think P figured the only way to get ahead of me was to go to Asia for a few years. While he was there they made him a vice president. When he came back to Canada his head had grown very large. He was a rising star within the organization, and I was not. I didn't make the sacrifices he did; I stayed on the continent.

While he was gone I developed a sourcing role within the organization that we called Customer Solutions. I was always looking ahead and I figured our sophisticated customers in the electronics industry would demand this. I mean, if I were them, I would—I would want to control my costs and keep up to date on the changing supplier/technology front. So through a series of events we created this customer facing supply chain. Again, I didn't play the politics right and they brought P back to run it.

Every year we did this survey called a leadership survey. It was a survey that your subordinates filled out, and it ranked you on your ability to lead. I scored a 95%. That was great. P scored a 13% and he was my boss. In fact the whole organization scored less than

50% and our department scored less than 40%. I got a call from the folks in human resources and they told me that they didn't know what I was doing there, but whatever I was doing, keep doing it. I felt good until P said one day, "I think we need to get a corrective action to human resources on how we are going to get you up to 100%. I said to P, don't you think it would be better if I helped you figure out how to get your extra 87 points, so you can get to 100? That wasn't politically correct, I know, but facts are facts. P would have never had the balls to fire me because, well, he doesn't have any, but you remember old T, the German. Well, he was ready to retire and ready to show his vindictive side. See, you can never beat the Germans; just ask the boys at Chrysler.

The German personal psyche is a subject for another book or article, because there is not enough paper in my office right now to start on that. But let's just say, they will get you in the end. So I got downsized. A lot of folks were surprised, but I was not. You see, I never had any success managing up. To me that meant sucking up, and I just wasn't going to put myself in that position. Remember, I said I would do the opposite just to piss them off. So I found myself on the street again, trying to pick up the pieces of my career.

Politics plays a big role in the organization. If you can find an organization that minimizes politics and divisiveness, you have a chance to grow and prosper. The Business Directory defines organizational politics as, "The pursuit of individual agendas and self-interest in an organization without regard to their effect on the organization's efforts to achieve its goals." These guys were masters of office politics and its vindictive uses, and it makes me often wonder how much more successful the organization would have been if the organization were truly empowered. But it was just another organization that rewarded conformity.

John P. Kotter, who wrote *Power and Influence,* says, "Important changes that are shaping the nature of work in today's complex organizations demand that we become more sophisticated with respect to issues of leadership, power, and influence." If you can limit office politics, interesting and inspiring dynamics will soon appear within the organization.

After a year of consulting, which, by the way, was really cool because I did a project for a door and window manufacturer who wanted to outsource their product to China. The reason I say it was cool was that I also looked at automating their processes, and actually recommended that they automate the process for making the windows. Long story short, I convinced them to automate rather than outsource. Then I got a call from a headhunter about an opening in Michigan to lead a supply chain development project. I really wanted to lead a team again, and as a consultant you typically don't get much of a chance to do that. That was really important for me.

Well, I should have known this opportunity was a loser. I mean, all the signs were there. This was a very large conglomerate in Michigan. The founding family still had managing interest in it and were very adept at running it into the ground. When I say all the signs were there, I mean that in the office of the director of human resources there was a computer monitor the likes of which I had never seen. This monitor had an 8 inch screen and the back end of it must have been three feet long. The first day I arrived at my office, the floor was covered with the most god-awful tile you have ever seen. I think I saw this pattern at a polka hall in Cleveland once. You know, the kind of stuff that they used in the early fifties. My desk was about 800 pounds, and made from nice hardwood, but it had never seen a spray of Pledge or a dust rag. The outside of the offices had those old partitions made of steel and the filtered glass on top and the hallways were full of those rugs you get from

Cintas. I called my wife and told her that if I ever
wanted to know what it was like before I was born, I
did now. I was going backward instead of forward in
my career. All the signs were there, but I didn't pay
attention to them.

My interview with the old man that ran the
company had nothing to do with the position I was
hired for, but instead consisted of a two-hour
dissertation on how to design tooling to make c-
clamps on a disa-matic molding machine in a foundry.
Always the process engineer, I aced that interview. In
the interview they had talked to me about becoming
the president of one of their divisions, but Generation
Four of their family was running that into the ground,
and soon after I arrived, I realized that that division
was going to be sold off in parts or go bankrupt.
(Generation Four was a complete buffoon and liked
to compare his family to the Fords. I will give the
Fords credit, because they got out of running Ford
Motor Company years ago, which is probably why it
is still there and very profitable.) The painful
turnaround that never turned around lasted 18
months before the ax fell. I was coming back from a
business trip in Brazil (where, by the way, we had
saved almost 1/3 the cost of a shipping container
around the world, and my secretary said that the head

of human resources wanted to see me when I returned. That is never a good sign. The day it happened, the CEO (again a ball-less leader) decided he would have one of his minions do the dirty work, and he wouldn't show up at the office. Sweet justice did prevail a few months later, when the board removed the father and son, while the sheriff stood by. That's how I know there is a God.

So I went back to the consulting world again for some very exciting stuff, until one day I received a call from an old subordinate in Michigan. Would I be interested in an opportunity in the mining products world? The economy was going great, but these guys could not figure out how to grow their business in conjunction with the growth in the wind energy sector. I figured it was a rather unsophisticated business, and I figured I could lend it some sophistication. But you know, again, if it doesn't smell right, it is probably spoiled. My strategy at this company went great for three months, but as soon as the economic downturn hit, they retreated. See, this was not a progressive management group, and mining or mining equipment companies never are. You can throw gas and oil into that category for that matter, as they are the same.

I told the CEO that this was probably the most
reactive organization I had ever seen; it wasn't the
least bit proactive. It is not good to be entirely
reactive. A blend of 50/50 is best. If you are at least
somewhat proactive, you don't need to be as reactive.
Sounds simple, doesn't it? Tell that to a bunch of
sixty somethings that have spent their whole lives in
mining. There is no enlightenment there. As soon as
the economy started to tank, they did what they did
best and reacted. That meant downsizing the
organization.

There are two things that I do know: once the market
tanks, you had better figure out how to get
competitive and land some new business, or you can
just take your ball and glove and go home. The last
things I would cut would be sales and supply chain or
sourcing. I would increase my sales effort, and I, as
the CEO or president of that business, would get my
ass on the road and close some deals. The second
thing I would do is cut my costs through the supply
chain. Now, more than ever, you need a leader in this
area. I hate to generalize, but engineers in their mid-
sixties who have risen to become presidents of
mining equipment companies can't really be classified
as "visionaries." Remember, these guys crushed rock,
and crushing rock has not changed in the last seventy

years. You just have too many things going against you there. The problems lie not only in their age, but also in that typically engineers aren't very open minded or progressive, and the fact that the mining industry itself needs a good kick in the ass to get out of 1950.

So business slowed to a crawl, and there were no orders for capital equipment, so naturally, I got the ax again—but this time, with a twist. Remember, I have said throughout this dissertation that are leaders are don't have any balls...well, I am traveling back from Milwaukee and I get a message on my phone to give my boss a call right before the fourth of July holiday. So not only does he fire me by phone, but he does it before a holiday, and he doesn't give me details as to what it means. Again, they refer me to trusty old human resources. But the human resources guy has some couth and he does not call me while on holiday. So just to really piss them off, I show up for work on Monday (I mean, really, they did not tell me when my job was going to be eliminated), and when I come in the front door the boss leaves through the back door. If you make a decision, fine, but at least have the balls to face up to it. This guy has finally retired, so the business world is relieved of one more problem.

A quote from a United Technologies advertising campaign in a 1980s *Wall Street Journal,* which I have had on my office wall for years, tells the story:

> Sometimes the decision to do nothing is wise. But you cannot make a career out of doing nothing. Freddie Fulcrum weighed everything too carefully. He would say, "On one hand...but then, on the other," and his arguments weighed out so evenly he never did anything. When Freddie died, they carved a big zero on his tombstone. If you decide to fish—fine. Or if you decide to cut bait—fine. But if you decide to do nothing, you're not going to have fish for dinner.

It takes a lot to be a leader. It takes conviction and fortitude. It takes a strong will and the ability and desire to do what is right. A leader sticks up for the small guy. A leader makes the choices that are right and not always the right choices. The examples I showed you in my life have all been learning experiences for me. I have had many teachers. Most have not known they were acting as teachers, but each taught me right from wrong and each led by example. Now, wouldn't it be a perfect world if it were meant to happen that way? Wouldn't it even be a better world if our leaders had "balls"?

This is reason number seven why our organizations are dysfunctional.

CHAPTER 8:
WHY OUR MBAS FAIL

The Dysfunctional Organization

Chapter 8

Up front, there are a couple things I would like to say about this chapter. First, it's not only our MBAs (Masters in Business Administration) that fail us. It's also our school systems that are failing us. My friend and I were having this discussion over dinner one night, and he made the point that not everyone is cut out for college. I believe he is right. However, we do not have the appropriate facilities to teach solid working skills to the masses. For example, the trades all work with an apprenticeship system, and though I believe those could probably be stronger, we do need an equivalent outlet for our next generation to pick up the skills they need in the new manufacturing arena.

Fab Labs tells us that,

> In the face of current economic challenges, today's manufacturing industries are employing Advanced or Next Generation Manufacturing tools, techniques, and technologies to survive. Fab Labs, developed by MIT, provide an ideal means for students to learn these next generation manufacturing skills. Successful next-generation

manufacturers will need to respond quickly to customer needs by rapidly producing customized, inexpensive, and high-quality products. This will require fabrication capabilities that can be quickly reconfigured to adapt to changing production and that can be operated by highly-motivated and skilled knowledge workers.

Next generation manufacturing technicians need to possess radically different skills than those needed in traditional production manufacturing. These technicians must flexibly translate imaginative and innovative design ideas into commercial products in just a few iterations. They need the skills to flexibly adjust their designs to just-in-time supply chains and resource availability with a minimum of waste. And they must be able to work in teams both within the company and in extended collaborations outside the company, even globally. Lastly, they must thoroughly understand and apply advanced technologies while adopting emerging technologies to maintain their expertise."

Not only will individual manufacturing workers need these skills, but a broader societal devotion to STEM (Science, Technology, Engineering and Math) needs to be enhanced as well. The State of Ohio has established the requirements for STEM learning, and other states are following the same path. This path is not only applicable at the high school level, but the college level as well. The State of Ohio model calls for the following:

- Engaging the public and private sector to design, start-up and operate STEM teaching and learning systems.
- Doing business through a portfolio of contributors and users who actively collaborate for the benefit of the whole.
- Pushing the envelope of education systems design to solve the complex problems in education.
- Creating a positive experience for STEM as it relates to education, economic development and personal prosperity.

These programs, once in force, will be greatly beneficial to America regaining some manufacturing positioning.

Now onto our featured topic: MBAs.

In an article for *CBS News*, writer and entrepreneur Penelope Trunk (2010) argues that the much-touted Holy Grail of business education, the MBA, is actually a waste of time and money. Pointing to all of the business school graduates struggling to find employment during the recession, Trunk offers the following reasons to support her thesis:

- Business schools won't help you be a good entrepreneur.
- You likely don't need an MBA for what you want to do.
- MBAs who are not from a top ten school do not increase their earning power.
- It's pointless after a certain age.
- An MBA is too limiting.
- An MBA makes you look desperate.
- Business school puts off the inevitable.

Trunk paints a rather dismal picture of business education. Is the MBA worthless? Is even an undergraduate business education worthless? If so, is there something that we can do in order to redeem it?

Ineffective leadership is indeed the biggest problem in American corporations today. However, the root of the problem resides in education, especially higher education. So why do we fail our young people so much? Why do we have such pompous attitudes about higher education, and why are our professors more interested in filling their own needs than those of the students?

I have always nurtured a keen interest in education, not only personally, but for my children as well. I was slow to catch on. When I finally got my act together in my late twenties I went back to school. I chose a school that fit my needs—a small, private college with a weekend program that allowed me not only to continue my role as a parent but also as a learner. This is where I learned another life lesson: there is no substitute for experiential learning. We don't need walls. What we need are compassionate, caring educators who can do the job, as well as teach others how to do it.

At the school, I majored in business and minored in economics. One of my economics professors was a man named Steve Zabor. Steve made a lasting impression on me that has carried on throughout my life. I had registered for an econ class, and apparently I was the only one out of nine hundred students who had registered for this class. I fully expected it to be cancelled, but the school surprised me and we had the class anyway, one on one. Can you imagine that happening today? Sure, you can take a tutorial and work one on one with the professor, but this drove home one significant point for me: the school cared more about the relationship with the student than it did about money.

Years later, I came back to Youngstown, Ohio to start and move my career in a different direction. I went back to the state supported school in town to see where I could help. I ran into an old acquaintance who I had worked with years before in The American Production and Inventory Control (APICS) chapter in Youngstown, and who was now chair of the management department, and I told him that I would like to teach part time there in order to give a little back to the career that had treated me very well. The school's thought was to teach the standard operations classes that they have offered for years, while my thought was to do something out of the box and bring the school into the 21st century. I sat in some of the classes, and believe me when I say I thought it was 1976 again. They were teaching (if you can call it teaching) materials I haven't used in business for the last 30 years.

My God, what a struggle. I know I learn best by doing, so I wondered what could we give the students that the out-of-touch staff couldn't offer. I came up with a little MBA class called Operational Projects. Operational Projects was a class that gave the students hands on learning in a consulting environment. In this class the students learned how to talk to businesses about their operational issues. They learned how to access their problems, come up with alternative solutions, and give them alternatives to think about in order for them to improve their operational efficiency. It was a success, although not supported well by the school, because the school really didn't understand it.

See, I think the world changes, but those who have made a career out of education think it remains static. Many of the students who took the experiential class told me it was the best class they had ever taken in their entire educational experience, and that they had learned a lot of practical applications for material they had previously learned. Many suggested we make it a "capstone" of the MBA program. The school could not really accept it, the dean did not understand it and did not support it, and so today, the MBA program at that school continues to lose enrollment by 10% per year and continues to offer the students far less value than it could. Why? There is a thought out there in the marketplace that MBAs should be taught by practitioners rather than education bureaucrats. I could not agree more.

The fact is, this idea is not new in the world of academia. One of the most prominent management thinkers to emerge from the world of education is Herbert Simon. Most widely known for his theory of "satisficing," Simon was also an advocate for greater inclusion of practitioners in the classroom. In a 1967 article for *The Journal of Management Studies*, Simon writes, "The typical business school faculty member, however, even on the applied end of the faculty, will not be a man with much or any experience as a manager. He will be a man who has followed an academic career. We must provide ways in which he can get access to the business environment."

Think about this for a moment. Every marketing or sales class I have ever taken talks about listening to your customers. Give your customer what they want and you will have a customer for life. We all remember that from either marketing or sales, don't we? But see, even though marketing and sales are parts of the business curriculum, they don't happen to be universally applied, as principles, across the school of business. If you ask what your customers want, what will you find out? Customers want hands-on learning experience. They not only want to read the material and develop a complete understanding of the materials, but they want to be able to know how to apply those things as well. They want to be able to touch and feel what they learn.

One of the coolest department stores in the Midwest is a place called Von Maur. Von Maur has signs all over the store that say, "Please touch the merchandise." It is part of the selling process. You like the goods, you touch and feel the goods, you buy the goods. In education, you learn the material, you read about it, but you still want to touch it and feel it—in other words you want to experience it. The problem is, how can you experience it when the professor has never done it? Professors are bureaucrats who are accustomed to using the same lesson plans for the past thirty years, publishing a few minor articles every once in a while that make them "experts" in the subject.

By loading our businesses with a bunch of MBAs who are experts in spreadsheets and theories of constraints is a tremendous disservice to not only our businesses, but our students as well. So if what I say is true, where are our future leaders going to come from? That is the question we must ask ourselves.

The essential problem with business schools today is that they teach students how to follow orders rather than how to lead. Most Masters of Business Administration Programs are highly analytical in nature. They produce researchers and bean counters, not business decision makers. In January of 2000, a groundbreaking study published in the *Journal of Marketing for Higher Education* (Paranto, 2000) revealed employers' dissatisfaction with business school programs. The finding of the study revealed four key deficiencies in business school preparation for the workforce:

1. A lack of emphasis on leadership and interpersonal skills—the skills most highly valued by employers.
2. A developing students with well-rounded capabilities, such as general creative and critical skills. Skill sets of students seemed too narrowly-defined and applicable to too few situations.

   A curriculum that lacks the most currently valued core competencies of businesses operating in the world today. A consistency in the quality (or lack thereof) of graduates coming out of specific schools.

So, why does this happen? Why are employers dissatisfied with business school graduates? As you might guess, my theory is that it has little to do with the quality of the students and more to do with the quality of the teachers.

It's not that business school teachers are bad teachers; it's more that they are equipping their students for the wrong profession. They aren't teaching their students how to become business decision makers—they are teaching them how to become researchers. In American corporations today, we don't need people who know how to study; we need people who know how to make decisions.

Should PhDs be teaching MBAs? My answer is an emphatic, "No!" To create Masters of Business Administration, we should be employing business administrators as teachers. But we're not. Instead, we're employing business theorists. We're allowing people to teach our future business leaders how to become better students, when what we really need are better leaders. In today's business schools, MBA doesn't really stand for "Masters of Business Administration." In reality, it stands for "Masters of Business Analysis."

The MBA needs to become more practical. We need more experiential learning. I'm not talking about going over case studies. I'm talking about working with local businesses to do real work. We shouldn't have our students merely *study* cases; we should have our students become *involved* in cases. As in any field, it's perfectly fine (and probably better) to have PhDs teach students who want to become business professors or researchers. But, for the vast majority, who want to get jobs making decisions in the real world, we need to employ more adjunct professors who are business practitioners to teach our business school students.

The success of business school attendees is measured in the same way as that of students in all other fields of academia: through quantitative testing. GMAT scores and GPAs determine a student's value. The problem is that there is no GPA for the real world. The marketplace doesn't care about your IQ. Yet, we train our business school graduates to evaluate themselves on the basis of arbitrary grades.

Seth Godin, (2012)in his educational manifesto titled *Stop Stealing Dreams* has this to say:

> Scientific schooling uses precisely the same techniques as scientific management. Measure

(test) everyone. Often. Figure out which inputs are likely to create testable outputs. If an output isn't easily testable, ignore it. It would be a mistake to say that scientific education doesn't work. It does work. It creates what we test. Unfortunately, the things we desperately need (and the things that make us happy) aren't the same things that are easy to test.

Those last words, "the things we desperately need aren't the same things that are easy to test," describe the problem facing business colleges today. We evaluate our students on the basis of their abilities to follow orders and get good grades, because it's easy. It isn't so easy to measure creativity, leadership, and interpersonal skills. Or, is it perhaps easier than we might think?

What if, instead of having our business school students take tests, we made them start businesses? What if we graded them on the basis of their failures and successes, not in the classroom, but in the marketplace? Think about it. Would you rather hire a new college graduate with a 4.0 GPA and a 750 GMAT score, but with no experience outside of the classroom, or a student with a 2.5 GPA and a 450

GMAT score, but who had actually built a successful, thriving enterprise? It's a no brainer, isn't it? We don't want workers who are compliant and can answer questions on tests. We want workers who are courageous and who can build businesses in the marketplace. Why aren't our business schools preparing their students for reality?

In an article for Forbes, columnist Eric Jackson (2012) points out the shock that students often face once they leave an MBA program and enter into the real world. Rather than being taught attitudes, behaviors, and skills that can make them employable, they often enter into the job market with beliefs that damage their chances of getting a position. Here are Jackson's ten most dangerous things students are taught in MBA programs:

1. That they actually matter because they have MBAs.
2. That they're the best of the best.
3. That they made a good investment.
4. That they're smarter than people without MBAs.
5. That the MBA will make them entrepreneurial.

6. That the MBA will have given them tools to understand the real world.

7. That they're okay if they've simply taken an ethics class.

8. That working on group projects made them team players.

9. That they should put the MBA on their business cards, as subtitles to their names.

10. That they will be great communicators because of the MBA.

Of course, the kind of education of which I am speaking would not be easy to implement. There are far too many political structures in place within academia to allow for that kind of change. And academia is the biggest part of the problem. But I do think that, in the future, alternatives to traditional education will arise that will put students into such scenarios. They might be more experimental academic institutions, or they might be professional continuing education firms, but either way, organizations will arise that will give students real world experience. It is inevitable, because our organizations need it. Imagine a program in which your tuition was used, not to hire professors to lecture to you, but rather to invest in capital and overhead for a startup. Does that seem far-fetched? Maybe it is. But, if our organizations are to become competitive again in America, it starts with the future of business education.

This is reason number eight why our organizations are dysfunctional.

CONCLUSION:
WHAT DO WE DO NOW?

The Dysfunctional Organization

<u>Conclusion</u>

So where does all this put us, and what do we do now to remedy the situation? We already have organizations that suffer from bi-polar tendencies. Do we all go out and hire organizational psychiatrists to solve our problems? Do we all get on the latest meds to make us happy?

We need to seriously take a look at the dysfunctions of all our organizations, prioritize the dysfunction by level of severity, and attack it. Think about it for a minute. We have little control over what our government does to support monetary policy, or do we? The issue of monetary policy is corrected at the ballot box. But the main question is, do the populace really understand the detrimental effect our current policy has on business today and how the undervaluation of our currency results in either an advantage for our economy or a disadvantage? Is manipulating our currency the way we do through the Federal Reserve Bank good or bad? When does the bubble we've created burst, and when does hyper-inflation set in? We have all been warned about the correction by now. If, and when, that happens, how are our businesses affected. We all know it will happen, but when? That is why, in 2014, there is such a tendency for businesses to hold on to cash and weather the next correction, because it could be major. Considering the Fed's policies, businesses are probably right to hold onto cash. You can't control monetary policy, but you can understand all there is to know about it and manage it.

Protectionist trade policies generally hurt business. Like I said before, if I am in the steel business and I deem I am at an unfair advantage, I am for tariffs, but nobody had better put the tariffs on automobiles or food, because I have to buy that and I don't want to pay more. So, we need to decide if it is in our best interest to become a free market society or a protectionist society. The French are a protectionist society. French automobiles are not really sold in huge numbers worldwide because they are expensive and of lesser perceived quality than those of the Germans. The French will not let their auto industry be destroyed by bringing in lower cost vehicles at the expense of their auto industry. They protect it. Here in America, we pick and choose just who gets the protection by how many congressional representatives it affects. It becomes a political game. In most cases, nations dump product into our markets at a cost that our producers can't match. What if the cost advantage the importers have is because we manipulate our currency to give ourselves an advantage? See how sticky this wicket is?

My advice is simple, we have great minds, great engineers and we should minimize whatever labor effect we have by automating, then we should let the politicos play their game.

We like Walmart, we really do, and if we didn't, we should have acted before all of the smaller business closed because of the superstore concept. The Walmarting of America is a simple problem, because the retailer is a byproduct of the mentality. My theory goes, "If you go to Wal-Mart and expect to pay less every time you go, your wages need to drop accordingly." My philosophy is, "I would expect to pay more every time, as I would hope my wages are rising more than the increased price I am seeing." Maybe there is something wrong with me, but this is just logical, right? Let's make sure we fully understand those cost implications before we buy. Let's make sure we really understand what offshoring does to the economy, and where we have labor cost issues, let's address them with automation. If we do that, our economy will prosper, not lag. Let's learn from the Germans and understand that labor and the human mind are precious things, and let's learn that we can, and should, empower people to make decisions about their own jobs going forward.

Let's not get into this trap of labor and unions. Union or non-union should not matter in 2014. Remember that labor union activity has fallen dramatically over the last 30 years. But also remember that we are in this era of non-union activity because of what the labor movement has done for our economy. The reason you have health care, vacations, and a forty hour work week is not because management was so forthright and generous. It is because labor unions, mostly through hard-fought negotiations, obtained these things for today's worker. Let's not create the mindset, as management, that we are smart, articulate people who, through our leadership, inspire people to not want to join unions. But let us remember that we are all people, and as such we should treat others as equals. If we do that, we will have labor harmony.

One other thing regarding labor: remember that the way to labor harmony is to get labor involved in the process. Whenever, I do shop floor turnarounds for companies, the first thing I do is walk the shop floor, interviewing all involved in the process, soliciting their ideas. What a novel concept, asking the people who do the job how to improve the job. See, this is a counterintuitive step to what I see in many cases. These are not robots. They are not folks to be looked down upon. They are contributing members of our organization that could either make us or break us.

One of the stories I tell my daughter continually is that no one wants to come into work and do a bad job. All of us want to do a good job and contribute to the success of the organization. We all have pride in ourselves and what we do. If their mission was to be destructive, we would know that after the first day. No one goes to work and says, "I can't wait to jam up that copy machine," or, "I can't wait to screw up that report." Why do people fail? It is because we, as leaders and managers in that organization, have not given them the opportunity to succeed. We control the tools, the communication, and the process for them to succeed. If we fail, we have failed as leaders and managers of our individual organizations in providing the opportunity for success. Don't look for blame when you fail, hold the mirror and check out who the real problem is.

You can control how empowered your employees are. Don't fall into what I classify as the "Age of Generic Management." Empowered work forces are dynamic, but remember, that does not absolve you from your obligation as a leader of that organization. I fact, if anything, it throws more responsibility on your back as the leader of your organization to provide the right type of culture to make an empowered team work effectively.

Dr. Patricia Arredondo of the Continuing Education Program at The University of Wisconsin-Milwaukee, says:

> So what exactly does it mean to empower people in the workplace? In *Successful Diversity Management Initiatives* (1996), she wrote that "Empowerment refers to a sense of personal power, confidence and positive self-esteem. Empowerment involves a process of change that can be achieved in relation to specific goals." Make no mistake, empowerment of self or others involves thoughtful planning, having actionable alternatives and of course, following through. Did I make the changes or succeed as desired?
>
> The term empowerment is not an all or nothing proposition; empowerment needs to be personalized and contextualized. It can mean giving a new employee support and guidance to meet their first six-month goals.

For mid-career professionals, it may mean ensuring they have the appropriate professional development and workplace experiences and exposure to move to the next level in the organization. For more senior employees an organization wants to retain, a sponsor may identify opportunities and lobby to develop the individual's talent with new assignments and perhaps other perks."

The future of American business will depend on almost exclusively on our willingness—our willingness to embrace risk, our willingness to empower our creative employees, and our willingness to shift from canned leadership to the inspirational leadership that our organizations need to lead America back to a competitive stance in the global economy.

Try to make your organization become one that inspires. Now, I have to be careful here, because I am not saying that you should try to make it an organization of leaders. To create that would be a mistake, because the organization will be going every way but forward. And let me add here, this is where you are probably going to need the most outside help. Leadership principles should be taught at every level of the organization, along with management and controls, along with the process for each of those things. You need to be clear about the expectations for each and every role within your organization. Brian Evje, in an article for *Inc. Magazine* says:

> The question is not whether leaders are born or made. Rather, we should ask what leaders have made of their attributes (inborn and otherwise), and which experiences they've had or missed. Leadership is learned because leaders are not born with special powers. They are made over time through challenges, personal courage, setbacks, self-reflection, and an ability to grow. Many leadership lessons require us to unlearn old habits, default reactions, and assumptions about human nature in order to adopt new and different choices and behaviors. This is not to say that anyone can lead; it is to say that true leaders learn over time.

He is telling us that leadership grows out of experience. He goes on to say,

A certain amount of learning takes place through observation, and a number of leadership elements can be demonstrated by good role models. However, there is a massive gap between seeing and doing. Too few people and organizations address this with deliberate, consistent, and constant leadership development. One particularly stubborn myth is that leadership is something one naturally gains over time, like graying hair. One survey of 17,000 global leaders found that the average age for their first leadership training was 42, "about 10 years after they began supervising people," and almost 20 years after they started experiencing leadership in organizations. That's a long time to observe leaders who are figuring it out on their own, while picking up their bad habits. A better approach is to take charge of the proper way to learn about leadership. What is more formal and serious than developing yourself, and what are you doing about it?

Let's build organizations of character and substance. No one would doubt that character and integrity are important in developing any kind of healthy relationship between individuals. However, most of us don't think that way in an organization's health. I would argue that it is very important. We need to get rid of the old myths and easy fallback we have always had as leaders and managers. Let's realize we are all on the same team, live by The Golden Rule, face up to our responsibilities, and not hide behind our positions. Let's be honest, truthful and inspiring. Let's have people follow us and aspire to be like us because we do the right thing.

I was recruited by a company that offered me a nice position, however it was dysfunctional, and the president and I weren't in the same decade, in terms of thinking. He was in 1940 and I was thinking, "How do I get this organization to even get to 2000 in 2008?" Either way, I was the loser in that game, and we parted company. When it came time to talk about severance, they offered two weeks. It was their policy to offer two weeks for every year someone was with the organization, and since they actively recruited me, I thought I deserved more. The HR Director agreed with me and said, "I really see your point, but I only have so much money to work with here." We settled on more, but in my mind, this organization wasn't full of substance and character, and I have a very low opinion of that organization today. No hard feelings, but a low opinion nonetheless. It is easy to do the right things in good times, but the true test of a great organization is that they do the right things all the time. That is tough to find today, but it is something that we should strive for as individuals, as well as corporate entities.

The final piece of all of this is to create a learning organization. Now this is in spite of all the roadblocks I mention in the book. I mention that we do not have the proper trade schools for our young people in America. I mention that our MBAs, for the most part, are impractical. They are taught by PhDs that lack practical experience and cannot implement anything that they teach in the classroom. Most of what I have learned in my life I have learned from actually doing.

I think there needs to be a tremendous shift to experiential learning. I think our educational system in America is more dysfunctional than ever and needs to go through a great overhaul, but good luck trying to get that one through. The way to combat our lethargic attitude is to make sure our organizations are learning organizations, where we foster cooperation, innovation, and creative thought, and reward people for thinking out of the box.

In the beginning of this conclusion I mention the concept of "Educate and Automate." The short solution for getting out of this mess we have created for ourselves is just that, short and sweet. We know what is wrong with our organizations. The question is, will we do something to move the needle? Will we put our pride on the shelf long enough to create a new, dynamic organization, one that has character, one that does the right thing? This needs to be one that inspires the individual to be creative and learn, as well as to be responsible. It needs to be one that you want to live in as well as hand down to future generations, an organization that will not only be competitive in this global market, but provide us with the ability to lead and prosper.

The Dysfunctional Organization

BIBLIOGRAPHY

The Dysfunctional Organization

Chapter 1:
How America's Monetary Policies Have Hurt Us

Trotman, A. 2013. "Fiscal Cliff as It Happened - December 31." *The Telegraph*, January 1. http://www.telegraph.co.uk/finance/economics /9772603/Fiscal-cliff-as-it-happened-December-31.html

National Debt Awareness Center. 2013. U.S. Federal Budget, Deficits, the National Debt, Social Security. http://www.federalbudget.com/

United States Mint. 2013. About the United States Mint. http://www.usmint.gov/about_the_mint/

Mankiw, G. 2011. *Principles of Economics*. 6th Edition. Cengage Learning.

Lehrman, L. 2011. The True Gold Standard: A Monetary Reform Plan without Official Reserve Currencies. The Lehrman Institute.

Lewis, N., & Wiggins, A. 2007. Gold: The Once and Future Money. Agora.

The Lehrman Institute. 2013. "Why the Gold
    Standard." *The Gold Standard Now.*
    http://www.thegoldstandardnow.org/why-the-
    gold-standard

Hoppe, H.H. 2011, November 14. "What's an
    Honorable Businessman to Do?" *LewRockwell.*
    http://www.lewrockwell.com/2011/11/hans-
    hermann-hoppe/whats-an-honorable-
    businessman-to-do/

Chapter 2:
Convoluted Trade Policies

Ricardo, D. 2010. *Principles of Political Economy and Taxation.* City: Nabu Press.

Friedman, T. 2005. The World is Flat: A Brief History of the Twenty-First Century. Firrar, Straus, and Giroux.

International Trade Commission. 2013. "The Harmonized Tariff Schedule." *Website Title here.* http://hts.usitc.gov/

Broyles, L. 2011. "GE CEO Challenges US Hiring Practices." *Digital Construction*, July 14. http://www.constructiondigital.com/innovations/ge-ceo-challenges-american-hiring-practices

Pettis, M. 2013. *The Great Rebalancing: Trade, Conflict, and the Perilous Road Ahead for the World Economy.* City: Princeton Univ. Press.

The Dysfunctional Organization

Chapter 3:
The Walmarting of America

Walton, S., & Huey, J. 1993. *Made in America*. City of
Publication: Bantam.

Fishman, C. 2006. *The Wal-Mart Effect: How the World's Most
Powerful Company Really Works--and How It's Transforming
the American Economy*. City: Penguin Books.

Morley, R. 2006, February. "The Death of American
Manufacturing." *Philadelphia Trumpet*, 17 (2): page
numbers here.

Madden, K. 2010. "America's 15 Most Popular Jobs."
AOL Jobs, November 11.
http://jobs.aol.com/articles/2010/11/11/americas-
most-popular-jobs/

"Average Manufacturing Salaries." 2013. *Simply Hired*.
http://www.simplyhired.com/a/salary/search/q-
manufacturing

Uke, A. 2013. "Buying America Back. Made in America
Movement." *Website Title goes here*.
http://www.themadeinamericamovement.com/buyin

g-america-back.html

"Why Made in USA?" 2012. *Made in USA Foundation.*
http://madeusafdn.org/about-us/why-made-in-usa/

"Made in USA Certified." 2013. *Website Title here.*
http://info.usa-c.com/

"Keeping America at Work." 2013. *Website Title.*
http://keepamericaatwork.com/

"Resources & Links." 2012. *Flag Manufacturers
Association of America.* http://www.fmaa-usa.com/resources_links/usflag_statistics.php

"Testimonials." 2013. *Annin Flagmakers.*
http://www.annin.com/testimonials.asp

Anderson, C. 2012. Makers: The New Industrial
Revolution. Crown Business.

Chapter 4:
The Labor Misperception

Becker, G. 1994. *Human Capital: A Theoretical and Empirical Analysis, with Special Reference to Education.* 3rd Edition. City of Publication: Univ. Chicago Press.

Drucker, P. 2006. *The Practice of Management.* City: Harper Business.

Gerber, M. 1990. *The E-Myth Revisited.* City:Harper Collins.

Laffer, A. and Peter J. Tanous. 2008. *The End of Prosperity.* City: Simon and Schuster.

Rotman, D. 2013. "How Technology is Destroying Jobs." *MIT Technology Review*, June 12. http://www.technologyreview.com/featuredstory/515926/how-technology-is-destroying-jobs/

Moore, S. 2009. "Missing Milton: Who Will Speak for Free Markets?" *The Wall Street Journal Online*, May 29. http://online.wsj.com/article/SB124355131075164361.html

The Dysfunctional Organization

Chapter 5:
The Loss of Individualism

Taylor, F.W. 2010. *Principles of Scientific Management*. City: Nabu Press.

Levy, S. 2011. *In the Plex: How Google Thinks, Works, and Shapes Our Lives*. City: Simon and Schuster.

He, L. 2013. "Google's Secrets of Innovation: Empowering Its Employees." *Forbes*, March 29: page numbers. http://www.forbes.com/sites/laurahe/2013/03/29/googles-secrets-of-innovation-empowering-its-employees/

Pink, D. 2006. *A Whole New Mind: Why Right-Brainers Will Rule the Future*. City: Riverhead Books.

Sinek, S. 2011. *Start with Why: How Great Leaders Inspire Everyone to Take Action*. Portfolio.

The Dysfunctional Organization

Chapter 6:
Where Have All the Leaders Gone?

DeBaise, C. 2009. "What is the Difference Between Management and Leadership?" *Wall Street Journal Online.* http://guides.wsj.com/management/developing-a-leadership-style/what-is-the-difference-between-management-and-leadership/

Hirsch, J. 2013. "Toyota Overhauls Management, Gives More Autonomy to North America." *Los Angeles Times,* March 6. http://articles.latimes.com/2013/mar/06/autos/la-fi-hy-toyota-management-overhaul-20130306

Iacocca, L. 2008. *Where Have All the Leaders Gone?* City: Scribner.

Surowiecki, J. 2005. *The Wisdom of Crowds.* City of publication: Anchor Press.

Prive, T. 2012. "Top 10 Qualities That Make a Great Leader." *Forbes,* December 19. http://www.forbes.com/sites/tanyaprive/2012/12/19/top-10-qualities-that-make-a-great-leader/

The Dysfunctional Organization

Chapter 7:
I Called to Tell You, "You're Fired."

Krawcheck, S. 2013. "The 7 Things I Learned When I Got Fired (Again)". *LinkedIn*, October 22. http://www.linkedin.com/today/post/article/201310 22115438-174077701-the-7-things-i-learned-when-i-got-fired-again

The Dysfunctional Organization

Chapter 8:
Why Our MBAs Fail

Trunk, P. 2010. "Why an MBA is a Waste of Time and Money." *CBS News Online*, August 18.http://www.cbsnews.com/8301-505125_162-45040152/why-an-mba-is-a-waste-of-time-and-money/

Simon, H. 1967. "The Business School: A Problem in Organization Design." *Journal of Management Studies*, 4(1): 1-16.

Paranto, S. R., & Kelkar, M. 2000. "Employer Satisfaction with Job Skills of Business College Graduates and Its Impact on Hiring Behavior." *Journal Of Marketing For Higher Education*, 9(3): 73-89.

Godin, S. 2012. *Whatcha Gonna Do with That Duck?: And Other Provocations.* Portfolio.

Jackson, E. 2012. "Dangerous Things Business Schools Teach MBAs." *Forbes*, August 26. http://www.forbes.com/sites/ericjackson/2012/08/26/the-ten-most-dangerous-things-business-schools-teach-mbas/.